PUPPY TRAINING

Best Tested And Fast Techniques To Train Your Puppy in Obedience, Potty Training And Crate Training

Ron Reynolds & Alexa Myers

Table of Contents

Chapter 11: Correcting Your Pup for Unwanted Behaviors

Prevent Jumping
Stopping Mouthing, Biting, and Nipping
How to Stop Destructive Chewing
How to Stop Excessive Barking
How to Stop your Puppy from Digging
How to Stop Excessive Urination
Curbing Aggressive Behavior
Stopping Your Pup's Separation Anxiety
How to Stop Obsessive Dog Behavior
How to Stop Hyperactive Puppy Behavior
How to Stop Your Puppy from Being Distracted on Walks
How to Curb Persistent Fear and Anxiety

Chapter 12: Advanced Obedience Training

Stand
Training Your Pup to Ask to Go Outside
Go To "Place"
Sit on the Street Corner
Shake (Body)
Stop
Touch
Back Up
Drop It
Leave It

Chapter 13: Bonus Chapter: Teaching Your Puppy Tricks

Hug
Dance
Balance
Rollover
Sit Pretty
Play Dead
Catch
Speak
Shake Paws

Conclusion

Introduction

Animal shelters across the world are filled with animals. Some people changed their minds, others may have moved and not been able to take their pets, some of the animals are strays, and others were not taught the right behaviors and their owners became exasperated and sent them away. One of the most upsetting things in this scenario is pet owners who adopt a puppy only to send it away when it tears up the house or they have problems housebreaking it. While training a puppy can be difficult, doing it correctly the first time will prevent scenarios like these.

You should remember that you only get one shot at training your puppy the correct way. Your pup will make associations toward behavior and reactions as soon as any type of training is started. While there is more than one technique that can be used for what your pup must be taught, doing it properly is essential to preventing bad behavior. This book will teach you to do just that.

Even when dealing with older puppies, however, you will still find it useful to follow the same schedule. An older pup may come with its own set of bad behaviors that it must unlearn. You will still find that you need to teach your puppy respect and then you will be able to correct the bad behaviors.

This book will teach you all that you need to know to teach puppies, young and old, how to behave as a member of your household. While you will find yourself faced with challenges and with obstacles to overcome, enough time and perseverance will allow you to teach your new puppy anything.

Best of luck training your new pup!

Chapter 1: Stages of Puppy Development

If you have ever taken a basic psychology class, then you know that babies and children go through stages when they are young that can influence their behaviors as an adult. Puppies are very much the same. They go through stages based on their age. In each, they are incredibly impressionable to certain types of training. This chapter will go through the stages of puppy development.

Birth to 7 Weeks

Most puppies wean from their mother at about 6 weeks of age. For this reason, it is likely your puppy will be a little older when they come home. Keeping your puppy with his mother and littermates during these first seven weeks is critical to training success. This is because the first seven weeks of your pup's life is a learning process where puppy will learn appropriate ways to seek attention, bite inhibition, how to follow leadership, and how to interact with other dogs.

If your puppy is not fortunate enough to learn these types of behaviors this young, they may be at an advantage when it comes to training. Though it will take longer, you should not be discouraged. The puppy will be able to learn these later if the right conditions are introduced.

7 Weeks to 8 Weeks

It is generally agreed upon in the dog community that puppies should go to their new homes at this age. This stage of development is when your puppy will form its strongest bonds with people. Additionally, they have reached the age of mental maturity when they can handle being separated from their mother and littermates. While your pup will probably cry the first few nights in her crate, she will adapt to her new lifestyle soon. This is also the age where you will want to begin teaching basic manners, though a lot of training will not yet stick at this age.

It is also during this period that you should start dominance training, being sure that your dog respects you as the authority in the home. You can do this by exerting your control and value in their life, such as making them wait for a moment to eat their food. More techniques for this will be discussed later in the book.

8 Weeks to 10 Weeks

Positive experiences are critical during this developmental period, which is the fear period of your pup's life. You will find that your puppy starts to make associations to objects and even people. If you yell at your puppy a lot or hit it, it will leave permanent imprints from which your puppy may never mentally heal. For this reason, interactions with you, other humans, your pets, and other animals must be as positive as possible to raise a mentally healthy pup.

You do want your puppy's interactions to be mostly positive, but you also do not want to allow him or her to get away with bad behavior. You can prevent bad behavior by keeping puppy on a leash until he is older or keeping him in a crate when you are not supervising him. If you must correct puppy, do so gently as you will learn later in the book. You should never hit or yell at your puppy to get him to behave, as it will probably have the opposite effect.

You should note that particularly scary or painful experiences can still damage your pup up to 12 weeks of age. If you cannot avoid something (like needing veterinary care or getting shots), then associate the experience with a positive reaction from you. Try to cheer your puppy up when he is scared, by praising him, laughing, or even acting like you are playing a game. Even though your reaction may be to soothe your pet, your pup will interpret this as and upset for you. This makes him anticipate that what is to come will be awful.

2 Months to 4 Months

By the time your puppy is 2-3 months old, you are going to want to start housebreaking them and teaching them other commands. At this age, their bodies have often matured enough that they can exercise control over their bodily functions (though smaller breeds tend to take longer). Additionally, they will have the mental maturity to sit through a training session and associate good behaviors with positive rewards and bad behaviors with negative consequences.

At this age, you really want to work on socializing your puppy so he is not afraid when he comes into contact with strangers and other animals outside of your home. Expose him to many different races and ages of people, introduce him to other animals, and let him explore the world to an extent. Make sure that you keep your puppy leashed, as he can easily become scared and try to run away. This can be disastrous, since your pup likely will not have master the come command yet.

4 Months to 6 Months

If your dog were a human, this would be considered the pre-teen stage of her life. You will find that your puppy is now more independent and that she shows confidence. This is especially true if you have properly socialized her with the world outside your home. You will also find puppy venturing farther from your side as you walk. You can allow this to an extent, but do not allow pup to pull.

Continue to train your puppy and emphasize lessons that you have already learned. You will want to be strict with your pup, because the next stage can be a rebellious one. If you are not raising your puppy for breeding, it is recommended that you spay or neuter them by 6 months of age as well. This will not only prevent you from having to raise a litter of puppies, but it will prevent hormones that can interfere with your dog's life.

6 Months to 12 Months

In this puppy development stage, your pup has grown into an adolescent. Your teenage dog acts much like a teenage child, defiant and ready to see how far boundaries can be pushed. You will also find that your dog is now incredibly active. Most dogs at this stage have a very high energy level and they will need activity, stimulation, and constant companionship to keep them out of trouble.

Even when your puppy is getting the activity he needs, you may find that he is disobedient during this time. Do not train in unsafe areas, as puppies can be unpredictable at this age. Continue to obedience train your puppy and do not let any bad behaviors slide, because if you do your dog will likely develop a related behavioral problem in the future.

12 Months to 18 Months

This is the time period when your puppy is going to age into a dog, reaching full emotional maturity. You will find that larger dogs take longer to mature than smaller breeds. You will also notice that your dog tries to become more dominant, as they try to rise in the ranks in your household. If you notice dominant behaviors, you must control them immediately to prevent future behavioral problems. Be sure not to react with punishment, however, because this will likely trigger aggression that may lead to a dangerous encounter with your pup.

Now that you have an understanding of the way that puppies develop into young, emotionally mature dogs, you are ready to learn what will be taught at each stage. The next section will outline a schedule that should be followed to ensure your puppy grows into a well-mannered dog.

Chapter 2: The Puppy Training Schedule

For some new puppy owners, the first thing they think should be addressed is housebreaking. This, however, is not farther from true. For your puppy to adapt well to his new life and learn to accept your authority and follow your rules (including his later training), it is important to start training your puppy from the first day that it sets foot in your home. This chapter will go over the puppy training schedule that you should follow, so you can be sure your pup learns everything that it needs without becoming overwhelmed. In the next chapter, you will learn about the attitude that you should hold and what steps to take to ensure that your pup sees you as the authoritative figure of the household.

Why a Schedule is Important

It can be very easy to get caught up in the excitement of a new puppy and try to teach them everything at once. Doing things out of a certain order can be confusing for a new pup though, especially when they are just trying to learn their surroundings. Additionally, teaching your puppy too much at once can overwhelm them and cause them to forget everything you want them to learn. To prevent this, you should adhere to a schedule that will help establish a routine, teach them some language, and then later allow you to housebreak them, teach them to be obedient, and more.

The Puppy Training Schedule

To be sure that you are not overwhelming your new addition, follow this schedule. If your puppy seems to take longer than others, do not worry! Simply delay teaching the new tricks until your pup is ready.

Daily Routines

The first thing that your new addition should learn is the daily routines that he or she will follow. You can do this by introducing your puppy to different areas of the house. You will want to pay close attention to:

- Where food and water dishes can be found

- When food will be provided

- Where your pup will go to the bathroom

- Where toys will be kept

- Where he or she will sleep

- When your puppy will sleep and wake up

As you show your puppy his or her daily routines, it is incredibly important that you use the right attitude and technique. You will learn more about this in the next chapter, so be sure to read it before you bring your pup home.

Gentleness and Acceptance of Being Handled

When you bring home a new furry pet, it is very likely that your family is going to want to hold and handle him. This is when you must first teach gentleness, so that your pup does not nip or scratch at your family members (or guests). You will find that some puppies need more training in this area than others, depending on their age when they come home. Often, their mothers and siblings teach them what is an acceptable amount of roughness when the pups play. It is important that you pick up where their mother left off in order to teach proper restraint.

Another related lesson is acceptance of being handled. There are times that you are going to need to do things your pup will not necessarily enjoy, including putting on their harness or collar, cleaning teeth, clipping nails, brushing, bathing, or giving medication. These are activities made much easier when your puppy stands still and cooperates. Teaching your puppy to accept you as a leader, from the beginning, will help them learn to be handled.

Language Basics

Before you can teach your puppy what behaviors are acceptable or unacceptable, you must teach them basic language. The easiest place to start is with commands like

No, which will signify that your pup should stop whatever they are doing in the moment and Good, which works to praise pleasing behavior.

Your puppy will be ready to learn these basics around 2-3 months of age. Pay close attention to your body language and tone of voice. This will continue to establish your role as leader in the household and your pup will listen to you as a result. It is essential that your puppy learn these words before you will even be able to consider any form of behavioral or obedience training.

Basics of Training

Once you have taught your pup the language basics, you will be able to teach them other acceptable and unacceptable behaviors, as well as housebreak them, crate train them, and more.

Crate Training

Some people frown upon putting a puppy in its crate, mostly because of the stories of owners who leave their pooches caged for long hours. When used properly, however, your puppy will begin to think of the crate as a safe area. You may find hat the pup even sneaks in there to nap or get away from the chaos of the household.

In addition to being your puppy's safe haven, you will find crating is useful for putting your pet away when you are out of the house or to take him or her on trips in the car. Additionally, it will be incredibly helpful when it is time to housebreak your pup.

Housebreaking

When puppies are new, they may still have trouble controlling their bowel movements so you should expect accidents when you first bring your pup home. Larger breeds often develop control at 2-3 months of age while smaller breeds need a little extra time. Even though you should expect accidents, however, you cannot ignore them completely. You want to teach your puppy that using the bathroom in the house is bad from the very beginning to prevent a habit from developing that will be a nightmare to break. You will learn about the many methods of housebreaking later in the book, so that you know how to get your pup started off right.

Basic Household Rules

In addition to all the things that are essential for pups to learn, it is important that you also establish household rules. While things like tearing up the toilet paper, going to the bathroom in the house, and getting into the trash are obvious no-no's, you must also consider specific rules that will be implemented in your house. Some of the things that you should consider include:

- Whether or not your dog is allowed on the furniture

- If your puppy is allowed to jump on someone's lap if they are sitting

- If your pup is allowed to bark at noises (most likely, no)

- Whether your pup may be present when you are preparing meals (this can be dangerous if something he cannot eat gets dropped, but it is up to you)

- If puppy can take toys away from kids or other pets (probably not because it can lead to dominance issues later)

- Whether or not he or she is allowed to eat table scraps

In addition to this list, you may find that you must set other guidelines for your puppy. The key to any set of rules is consistency. If you live in a large family, consider making a list of unacceptable behaviors and ensure that the puppy is corrected the same way for infractions. Additionally, be sure that all of the rules are enforced.

Adapting Your Training as Your Puppy Develops

Training your puppy is something that you are going to be working on for a long time, from their early days as a new part of your family to their tough adolescent years to training a full-grown dog. At each step, you will find there are techniques that work better than others.

When you dog is a puppy, it is critical that you do not let anything slide. There will come a day when your puppy may be able to sleep in your bed or be trusted alone in the house, but their puppy days are not it. When your dog is a pup, the key is establishing your position as a pack leader. You also must be firm with your pup. Do not make excuses for bad behavior like nipping by justifying it because he is teething. Allowing any bad behaviors to slide is a recipe for disaster. Additionally, teach that you are the source of your dog's playtime, food, and other resources. This gives you value to the pup as a pack leader, which will be an important tool to curbing the rebellion of the adolescent stage.

Adolescent dogs are just like human teenagers. They are pushing their boundaries and testing limits, constantly questioning why they must listen to you when they would much rather be doing something else. The only thing that you can do to prevent bad behavior in this stage is to be firm with the rules that were established. Do not let bad behaviors slide- there will be time to let your dog sit on your lap or sleep with you, but it is not while they are still learning their place in your household.

The good news is that once you overcome your puppy's stage of teenage defiance, they will grow into a dog that knows what is expected of him or her. Additionally, you will now find that you are even close to your dog. They will look to you as a leader and then they will look to you as a close companion, as training strengthens your bond. You should continue any behavior-based training that you have not completed yet at this stage, but you will also want to place a lot of emphasis on games and activities to keep your dog's mind and body active. The adult stage is also when you can start to use biscuit training and teach your dog more advanced tricks, if you choose.

What If You Adopt an Older Pup?

As you read the chapter above, you may have noticed that it was recommended that many behaviors be taught around the age of 2-3 months. While this is recommended, you will find that the training schedule for older pups is very much the same. You must establish respect as you teach them their routines. Then, they must learn the basics of good and bad before teaching the next set of behaviors. They will still learn the same way; they will just be older than new puppies.

Be Cautious with Biscuit Training

One of the biggest mistakes that new owners make is getting their puppy to do what they want by biscuit training them. While the occasional treat will not harm your relationship with your puppy, using biscuits as a means of reward teaches your puppy to only listen when he or she wants a treat. Then, if whatever they are doing is more appealing than a biscuit, they may choose not to listen to you at that time.

You will find that there is a time for biscuit training, especially if you want to teach your dog to do tricks. Rewards are also very useful for obedience training when employed correctly. When you bring them home, however, it is not the time for obedience training and tricks. Instead, work on respect training and teaching your pup good and bad behavior before you try using biscuits as incentives for training.

Now that you have an idea of the skills that you should be teaching your puppy and when, it is time to move on to exactly how to teach each behavior to your puppy. As you read on and learn to practice each step, it is important to remember that consistency is key, as is having your puppy view you with respect

Chapter 3: Preparing for Your New Puppy Before He or She Comes Home

You will find that the first few days your puppy is home are the most critical to setting the tone for the training that he or she will undergo for the rest of their life. This does not mean the basics that you will have for your pup, such as a collar and leash, bed, crate, food and water dishes, toys, and other items. Instead, preparing in this sense means getting your family onboard with your new family member's training.

To make it easier to train your pup, it must respect you as the leader in your home. It must also look to other family members with authority. While they may not be responsible for training, their role will be critical in ensuring your puppy's training success. This chapter will go over what you need to talk about with your family before you bring your pup home.

Responsibilities

Once you have made the decision to bring your puppy home, sit down beforehand and have a family meeting. Here, you should go over the responsibilities that everyone has in regards to the pup. This includes who will shut her away in her crate for bedtime (which is a good idea until she is housebroken), who will get up and feed the puppy in the morning, and which family members will be responsible for which part of the puppy's routines.

You will find that the person who is primarily training the puppy should be present at the many parts of the routine. This is especially true if you are trying to establish respect between yourself and your dog. While your puppy may eventually listen to the other members of the family as they are trained to, you will find that they will follow your leadership and guidance over that of others once they are properly trained.

Roles

In addition to your family members learning their responsibilities regarding the new puppy, they must learn their specific roles. For training to be successful, it is important that your pup regard you as the alpha in the home. Whether you are a male or female, the pup should look to you as the leader of the pack.

It is good to establish who will be the alpha in your pup's life. It is a good idea that the alpha is the person that the pup has most contact with, who will be responsible for most of pup's training. Additionally, you will want to establish dominance with other family members. Your puppy should eventually listen to each member of your family, especially when they are trying to get your pup to do something or must correct pup for something.

Consistency

After establishing each member of your family's responsibilities and roles regarding your new puppy, you must determine what rules will be placed into effect in the house. This is a good time to go over things like where puppy is allowed and when, if he or she is allowed to sleep with family members (discouraged at least until he is potty trained), and other basic house rules. You will also want to establish how puppy is corrected. If there are a lot of rules and you have young kids, you may find it helpful to make a list so everyone is clear on how pup will be trained.

Establishing a Routine

Being consistent with your pup and establishing a routine go hand in hand. You must remember that your puppy has been taken away from its siblings and mother, which can be a stressful situation. While there may be occasional whining during crate training at first, you will find that it is essential to establishing a routine. As your pup learns that the crate is its safe space and not intended for a punishment, you will find your pup more settled.

There can be many elements to a routine. For example, your puppy may be taken out of the cage in the morning and taken to the bathroom, then to eat her first meal of the day. Then, she may play for a while, use the restroom, and return to the cage for a nap. The day will continue in a similar way. Be sure that the same person feeds the pup at the same time each day and that the same person is responsible for walking at the same time. For example, mom may walk the pup in the morning and the kids may walk the puppy around the backyard when they get home from school each day. At this early age, you will find that a familiar routine will be comforting to your pup and take some of the fear away about being in a new home and away from his siblings and mother.

Don't Get Caught Up in the Excitement of a New Puppy and Stick to the Rules

If you want puppy training to be a success, you must start from day one. Imagine for a moment that you bring home a new puppy. Your entire family is excited and you even cave and let the puppy sleep with one of your kids for the night. Unfortunately, since pup is not yet housetrained, he goes to the bathroom in the bed. When he is locked away the next night, he will whine since he got his way the first night. This keeps the entire household up and your family is much less enthusiastic the next day, as pup kept everybody up and they are less likely to want to roll out of bed and feed him. This cycle will continue with all behaviors, as pup will try to whine until he finally learns that it will not always get his way. The easiest way to prevent this problem is to stop it before it begins and to remain consistent from the first day you bring your young pup home.

Tips for Kids and Puppy Training

For some parents, their biggest fear about bringing their puppy home is allowing it to interact with their children. They may fear that the kids will train the puppy wrong and make it more difficult to teach and prevent certain behaviors. Even if you are afraid of this, it is important that you

#1: Remember to Give Puppy Downtime

It is likely that your children will be the most excited about the newest addition to your family. Despite their excitement, remind them that puppies often sleep quite a bit because their bodies are still growing. Pay close attention to your puppy's cues. If he seems nippy or agitated, allow some quiet time for him to lie down and relax. Remember that the entire world is new to your puppy and overstimulation can make them agitated, as well as prevent them from getting the sleep that they need.

#2: Give Your Kids Their Own Set of Commands

If your kids are using the same commands that you are, it can confuse pup as to who is the leader of the home. Additionally, you may find that pup becomes confused about what they are supposed to do, especially if your kids are not training him or her the right way. To overcome this hurdle, the best thing you can do is give your children a set of commands to use that is different than your own. For example, instead of everyone telling your dog Come to get him or her to come over to you, the kids could use the word Here and you could use the word Come.

#3: Teach Kids to Turn Their Back When Pup Jumps

Other than allowing pup to come out of his or her pen when whining at night, the biggest mistake that puppy owners make is allowing him to jump up when he gets excited. This is especially true when he meets the kids, because they will be less likely to correct your pet. Instead of corrections, teach your kids to turn their backs on pup when he jumps up. Then, when he is seated, turn back around and offer praise.

#4: Be Sure That Your Children Know (and Follow) the Rules

Establishing a set of rules that everyone will follow is essential to proper training of your pup. In the earliest days, you will find that your kids will whine and even beg to break rules like letting the puppy sit on their lap on the furniture or letting her sleep in their bed. If you cave, however, you can undermine your puppy's entire training practice. Firmly remind your kids that the rules are in place for a reason and that it is your (and their) responsibility to ensure that the puppy grows into a well-mannered dog.

#5: Do Not Leave Your Kids Unsupervised with Your New Pup

Leaving children alone with a puppy is never a good idea. Even if you believe your children are mild-mannered, you will notice that your puppy can become overwhelmed very easily in its first week or so of being home. Since kids are less likely to pick up on your pup's exhaustion cues, you should supervise them at all times. This also a good idea in case your pup has not quite been taught gentleness, because he or she may nip at the kids if they become overexcited. Another reason never to leave your puppy alone with kids is because they may be too rough. This is especially true of young children, which may pull on the puppy's tail or ears. If you find your kids guilty of this, be sure that you remind them puppies are not playthings, regardless of how cute they are.

Tips for Teaching Your Spouse Proper Puppy Interactions That Won't Ruin Your Training

Sometimes, it is not the kids that you have to worry about when it comes to sabotaging your pup's training. You may find that your spouse is the biggest threat to all the work you have done, especially when they only interact with pup after they have been at work all day. Here are some of the most common problems you may encounter regarding your spouse and how to overcome them.

#1: They Sympathize with Pup and Bend the Rules

If you have been paying attention so far, then you know that one of the biggest factors in the success of your puppy's training is consistency. This means that when your partner feels bad for pup and they let her out of her cage to sleep in your bed or don't punish her for bad behavior, they are sending an inconsistent message. This will, in turn, make it harder for you to train pup.

Sit down with your partner and explain that it undermines your training and confuses the puppy. It also makes it harder for them to determine good behaviors and bad behaviors, which could lead to behavioral problems down the road.

Explain to your partner that training will not last forever and eventually, pup will know how to decipher good from bad and you can be more lenient. If they feel left out, give them a specific trick or command to teach pup.

#2: They Yell at Puppy

If you have a spouse who comes home after a long day at work and just does not want to deal with pup and her bad behaviors, you may find that they yell. It is likely your partner is yelling because they believe that louder volume equals power. Additionally, your dog may cower when being yelled at. If your partner is unfamiliar with dog training, they probably think this means pup is acknowledging his wrongdoings.

Talk to your partner about the proper way to discipline a pup. If they defend their methods because of the cowering, tell them that pup is cowering because he is afraid. Eventually, this fear may turn to aggression if pup decides to fight back against the anger. Pup may also start to ignore the yelling or act out, instead of behaving. Finally, tell your partner that instead, it would be best to use a firm voice and gentle correction to get your pup to learn unwanted behaviors.

#3: They Go Behind Your Back and Bend Rules

This type of personality is even harder to deal with than the sympathizer, because they flat-out do not care about your rules. They sneak around to let pup jump up on their lap or sneak them scraps under the table. While they may see this as a good thing because the puppy likes them, they likely do not understand the difficulties pup will develop with listening as a result.

If this happens, calmly explain to your partner that when they do this, they are undermining his training. Explain that your dog will not learn to listen, which will lead to bad behavior and even potentially dangerous situations for pup in the future. Finally, stand strong and tell them that you will not tolerate any more of their behavior and if they continue to undermine you, they will not be allowed alone with the puppy without your supervision.

#4: They Argue with Your Training Techniques

Some people feel as if they know everything when it comes to training a puppy, especially if they once watched a dog training show or owned a dog in the past. Explain to them that training is your journey, as you are the one primarily responsible for the puppy. Tell them that you would appreciate the space to do things your way so that training remains consistent. Finally, find ways to involve them in what you are doing so they have a better understanding of how the training process works.

A Few More Things to Remember

In addition to the rules for your puppy, the kids, and your spouse included above, there are a few other things that you will want to keep in mind when you bring your puppy home.

#1: Correct the Dog Properly

Hitting and yelling is never okay, no matter how frustrated your family members become with the new puppy.

Remember that your pup is young. When you yell or hit, you do little but cause confusion for your puppy. It even has the potential to damage your relationship (and pup's behavioral patterns) in the future because your puppy may develop trust issues.

#2: Feed Your Pup and Then Leave Him Alone

Anxiety while eating is something that can be very detrimental to your puppy's development. Hovering or kids trying to play with pup while he is eating can cause him to become anxious. In some cases, it can even lead to food aggression, which can cause your puppy to bite or growl when another pet or family member approaches them while they are eating. Instead, give your pup his food and then give him some peace as he eats

#3: Puppies Will Follow Their Instincts, Especially Chewing

It is essential that you take the precautions to keep your puppy from getting into too much trouble in the first few weeks. Remember that your puppy will rely on its instincts in its first few weeks in your home, as well as direction from you. Since they are not likely to learn your position as leader right away, be sure to keep electronics, shoes, and other chewable items out of your puppy's reach.

Once you have established the rules and set specific guidelines for your family to follow, you will be ready to bring your puppy home. Read on to the next chapter to learn about your pup's first few days in his or her new home and how to teach routine so that your pup views you as the leader of the home.

Chapter 4: Bringing Your Pup Home and Establishing Dominance- How to Teach Your New Puppy That You Are the Boss as You Teach Daily Routines

Have you ever had a fellow pet owner laugh about their pup's dominant behavior or joke that he or she only listened when they wanted to? While it's easy to laugh your puppy's behavior off, you will find that it makes it incredibly difficult to teach your puppy behaviors. The problem with a dominant pup is that he or she does not view you as the leader in the household. Therefore, you may have behavioral problems arise or find that your puppy only behaves and does what it is told when it is convenient for them. This chapter will teach you how to establish dominance so that your puppy knows from the start that you are the leader in your household.

Why Pack Leadership is Essential to Preventing Bad Behavior

One of the first things that you must learn when correcting your dog is that dogs are not intellectual beings. Instead of listening to reason, they are going to follow instinct. For the most part, chewing, lashing out aggressively, eliminating on the floor, and other bad behaviors are caused by your pup's instinct. The key to preventing these and other bad behaviors is to overrule your puppy's instinctual behavior with pack leadership. Since dogs are instinctually pack animals, learning to establish yourself as the dominant being in your house will help overcome any behavior problems that may arise as your pup grows and explores.

Technique for Establishing Pack Leadership at a Young Age

Step 1: Develop Confidence in Yourself

If you have never owned a puppy before, chances are that you may be nervous about the situation. You may find yourself even more worried about how you will housebreak puppy or how you will get him to view you as a pack leader. The first step to showing your dominance in pup's life is to be confident in your training. Be strong with your words and directions and believe that you WILL be able to train the pup. After all, if you are not confident in your abilities to be a pack leader and train your pup then your pup will probably pick up on your lack of confidence and be less inclined to follow your direction.

Be very cautious of approaching your dog with the wrong kind of energy. A good pack leader is calm, but assertive. When you project nervous energy, anxiety, or other emotions, your puppy will pick up on it. Be wary of your pup's behaviors, especially if they are chewing on their leash, pulling, or showing other signs of anxiety. If you notice them, reevaluate your own confidence and attitude and put yourself in check before interacting with your pup.

Step 2: Use the Right Body Language

Confidence is not only your attitude. It is also the way that you carry yourself and the body signals that you send when you are interacting with your pup. Always stand with an air of confidence, with your spine stretched and tall. Hold eye contact with your pup when you are speaking and be sure that your confidence is exuded with both your posture and the tone of your voice. This will help to convey to your puppy that you own the space where he lives and that you are of value to his well being. Establishing this type of relationship with your puppy will make it easier to train him and make him instinctually follow your rules.

Step 3: Walk Pup the Right Way

You would be surprised by how much using the right technique while walking will help your pup. Since puppies are little balls of energy, they will need walked at least once a day. For energetic pups, you may want to walk them more than this to help them get out their pent-up energy. When you walk your puppy, walk as though you are leading a pack. Do not let your dog control the walk. Instead, hold the leash taut as you walk, without choking the pup. When you walk in or out of the door of your home (as well as the gate, if you have one), be sure that your pup follows you and that you lead first. As you walk, keep your puppy either behind you or at your side. Do not allow pup to walk in front, as this is a sign of leadership.

When you walk your puppy, it is important that you decide how far you will walk and where puppy is allowed to walk (either next to or behind you). Remember that you are the one in control and use this to assert yourself over the pup. If he or she starts to misbehave, gently correct your puppy. Mothers will pick a pup up by the scruff of its neck to assert herself without hurting the pup; you can use the leash in the same way.

Step 4: Assert Your Leader Status with Control

There are things that your puppy is going to want from you, including food, toys, and attention. There are a few ways that you can use control to assert yourself as leader in your home. Here are two.

When you make your pup wait, you are asserting your status as leader in the home. Waiting can be used for anything that your puppy needs from you, especially food. When you feed pup, place the food bowl down and use a cue word (like go ahead) when you are ready for pup to eat. If your pup will not wait, pick up the bowl and set it on the counter. Wait a minute and try again. When you make pup wait (and work) to eat, you take another step toward controlling your puppy's life (and their behavior).

Another technique you can use is establishing control over your puppy's toys. Leave out 2-3 at a time, switching them out when you want to. If you give your pup too many toys, he may find a place to hide them from you in a show of dominance.

Step 5: Understand Your Puppy's Needs

When you first bring your puppy home, you will most likely have built a routine based on your pup's size, breed, and amount of energy you are expecting. With time, however, you are going to learn more about your puppy's sleep and bathroom schedule and how often he or she must eat to remain healthy. Once you have an understanding of your puppy's needs, don't be afraid to adjust the routine slightly to make them feel fulfilled in your home. Once you do find the right routine, however, be sure to stick with it. You will find that stability is key to keeping your pup happy and well behaved.

Showing the Pup Around and Establishing Routine

You are going to find that the easiest way to train your puppy is by keeping him on a leash throughout the house at first. This will keep pup chained to you, which is what you want when there is such a high chance of her learning bad behavior. The problem with bad behavior at this age is that it is nearly impossible to correct it. The best solution until your puppy learns language basics, therefore, is to keep your puppy in her crate or at your side at all times.

You are going to use the same techniques as you show pup around that you would while walking her. Hold the leash taut and guide pup, without choking her or dragging her around. Show your puppy her crate, where she can eliminate her waste, where her food and water are located, and where her toys are. As you go through the routine from day to day, use the same technique. Consistency will teach your puppy what to do and eventually you will be able to take pup's leash off.

Introducing Your Puppy to Your Family (People and Pets!)

The last thing that you want to do is surprise your new puppy and cause it to be afraid in its new home. For this reason, you (as the alpha) should introduce pup to each of the people who live in your home. Do this slowly, allowing time for your puppy to sniff each person and understand that they are okay. You should also introduce your puppy to other pets in the home, especially those like other dogs or cats that may roam. Give them time to smell and assess each other. Hopefully, knowing that the other belongs will the pets from fighting if they encounter each other in other areas of the house.

In an ideal situation, you will have time alone with the puppy before he or she is introduced to the members of your family. This will give you time to show pup around before all of the excitement ensues and make it more likely that your lessons will sink in.

Once you have established a routine and your puppy starts to respect your leadership, you will be ready to move on to other parts of training. The next few chapters will be broken up according to what you will be teaching your pup. In some sections, such as housebreaking, you will find several possible methods and you can choose what works best for you and your puppy.

Chapter 5: Teaching Your Pup Basic Language and Good Behavior vs. Bad Behavior

In addition to basic respect, the only thing that you will need to begin teaching your puppy household rules and basic commands is proper language. This includes a praise word (like good) and a word to discourage bad behavior (like no or bad). You will find that your puppy knowing the difference between being praised and being reprimanded is essential to learning other commands. Therefore, you will not be able to move on to other commands until your puppy learns the basics. Fortunately, the easy 4-step process contained in this chapter will allow you to teach your puppy the difference between good and bad behavior in any situation.

Step 1: Understanding Training with Positive Reinforcement

Positive reinforcement is a branch of operant conditioning, which conditions a subject to behave based on the introduction of a reward or punishment depending on their behavior. Since punishments like hitting your dog or yelling tend to trigger aggression more than they are effective, positive reinforcement is the preferred method of teaching your dog.

The thinking behind this type of training was studied by B.F. Skinner, a behaviorist and psychologist, in the 1940s. It was the 1990s when it was introduced as a method of dog training, as an alternative to training that relied on fear, dominance, and punishment. The advantage of positive reinforcement over more traditional methods is the increased strength of the bond between you and your pup, as well as an increased willingness to learn for no other reason than to please you.

The Key to Choosing the Right Rewards

If you were paying attention in the first chapter, they you likely noticed that biscuits are not a preferred snack to get your dog to behave. This is because they will likely only behave when they are presented with a biscuit. Despite this, offering a treat as part of training can be helpful if it is done in the right way. Additionally, you should remember that you can only offer your puppy rewards once they have learned to respect you as the leader in your home.

The rewards that you choose for your dog will depend on his or her own preferences. Some dogs enjoy training treats, while others prefer jerky or cheese as a reward. Try several different things on your dog and pay attention to what he enjoys most.

Establish a Hierarchy of Treats

Once you know what your dog enjoys, you should establish a hierarchy of treats for where your dog is training. You will find your dog will be more motivated to train in distracting environments (like the walking park) if they are rewarded with a treat they value more than the ones you typically use at home.

You should give the lowest value rewards in the house, since this is the least distracting area. Some good low-value rewards include praise, ice cubes, kibble, carrots, or green beans.

When you do training in the yard, your dog may be distracted by cars, squirrels, other dogs, and passing pedestrians. For this reason, give a higher-level treat like cheese, jerky treats, or training biscuits.

When you train at the park or somewhere else away from home, the unfamiliarity and busyness of the area is going to make it difficult for your puppy to concentrate without high levels of motivation. Some good options here include hot dog, deli meat, hamburger, chicken, or liver. Again, remember to rank the hierarchy of treats based on your puppy's preferences for the best results.

Considerations for Clicker Training

In some cases, puppy owners choose to use a clicker for training. This clicker basically rewards pup by telling her that she is being rewarded for the behavior related to the command that you have given. It also signifies that there is a chance to earn treats, since always keeping treats on hand may lead to a puppy that only wants to do what you ask when there are treats in sight.

#1: Keep Treats Well Hidden

One of the things that you should do as you clicker train your puppy is keep treats hidden. Have you ever heard someone say that their puppy only obeys commands when they can see a treat? When done the right way, clicker training prevents this because the clicker is related to the behavior instead of the treat. As you clicker train, be sure to keep all of your puppy's treats hidden in airtight containers so that pup cannot smell them. You can keep them nearby, provided pup does not see them. After you have rewarded your pup with a click for their behavior, go to your stash area to get the treat. Instead of relating the treat to the command, your puppy will relate the trick to the command that you are teaching.

As you read the rest of this book, particularly the sections on teaching commands and tricks, remember to click in the areas where it says treat if you are clicker training your puppy.

#2: Click Only for Rewards for Behavior, Not to Get Pup's Attention

As you clicker train your puppy, it is essential that you remember that you can only use the clicker to highlight behaviors that your pup is doing. The clicker should never be used to get your puppy's attention. The reason for this is that your puppy will relate the clicker with you wanting her attention, instead of relating it to the behavior she is performing. This can lead to confusion with your puppy and lead to difficult or even disastrous training sessions in the future.

#3: Always Follow a Click with a Treat

The key to success with clicker training is the positive correlations between a click and a treat. For this reason, it is critical that you always follow a click with a treat. This will strengthen the connection between a click and the behavior that you want. This will become increasingly useful as you teach more difficult tricks to your pup.

Step 2: Relate Praise with Good and Pleasurable Activities

Almost all puppies enjoy playing with toys. The easiest way to teach your puppy what constitutes good behavior is to praise him when he plays with or chews on his toys. When you bring your puppy home, show him the toys and if he is interested, offer plenty of praise, petting, and smiles. Then, use the words good dog or good boy (depending on what your chosen phrase is) to help relate the word good to this acceptable behavior.

Step 3: Be Sure Pup Knows He or She is Being Corrected

In the first few weeks, you should plan to spend a lot of time with your pup and to put him or her away whenever you cannot watch them. The reason for this is that you cannot correct bad behavior if your puppy is not caught committing the bad behavior. For example, imagine that you go into the kitchen to wash a load of dishes and leave puppy out. She sneaks into the bathroom and chews the toilet paper roll.

When you find the mess, puppy is nowhere to be found. A few moments later, you find her snoozing in her crate.

While your first reaction may be to snatch puppy from her crate and drag her toward the mess to correct her, this will cause harm to her training. Like human infants, young puppies have a very short attention span. If you wake pup from her nap to correct her, she may think that you are correcting her for taking a nap in the crate. This is true even if you show her the mess, because her brain will not be able to link the bad behavior of ripping up the toilet paper with the correction.

Step 4: Discourage Bad Behavior

When you do catch your puppy in the act, you should use a loud and firm voice to tell your puppy no or bad or stop. You must pay close attention to your tone of voice and body language as you correct your puppy, as this is essential to her learning that you are displeased with her behavior. You also must be careful not to yell or hit your puppy, however, because this can cause aggression in puppies. Though you do not want to raise your voice, you should speak in a much deeper tone than you normally would and be less friendly then you would to communicate your dissatisfaction.

Step 5: Reinforce Good Behavior

Once your puppy understands that you are displeased, ignore her for a few moments while you reinforce a good behavior. If you can, do the opposite of the bad behavior. If your puppy has used the bathroom in the house, for example, you will want to remove her to the appropriate area for her to use the restroom. If your puppy has been caught chewing something, you will take her to her toys. Ignore your puppy until she is in this area and then reward with plenty of praise once your puppy does the good, acceptable alternative to the bad behavior.

One of the easiest ways to start training your puppy is to distinguish acceptable behaviors from unacceptable behaviors early on. Relate these to keywords like good dog or bad dog so he or she learns what is expected. By following this simple routine, you can teach your pup the difference between good behavior and bad behavior. This is the foundation that you will need to have before you can start to build on their training and teach more advanced commands.

Chapter 6: Teaching Gentleness and Socializing Your Pup

One of the things that you will want to teach your puppy early in his or her life is how to interact with your family members, pets, guests in your home, and even strangers and dogs that they encounter outside of the home. Socialization, gentleness, and acceptance of being handled all go hand in hand. It will make it easier to interact with your pup, whether it is for playtime or because they need to be bathed or medicated.

Gentleness

When your dog plays, you may notice that she swipes at the toy, pretends to bike, and even barks. Unfortunately, these behaviors can become too rough when they are taught improperly. This can lead to injury for yourself, your family members, and other people or dogs that your pup may play with. You may or may not have to do a lot of work when it comes to teaching your dog to be gentle. Often, a puppy learns this skill while he is with his mother and littermates. When your puppy does not get enough of this training, you will find that you need to pick up where his training left off.

Discourage Rough Play

Often, puppies are not gentle when they are playing because they get over-excited. There are a few things that you can do to make sure your puppy is not rough when playing. First, only play with your dog with toys. Do not allow anyone to play with your pup using their hands, feet, or limbs. Second, spay or neuter your pet if they are not going to be bred. This will help discourage shows of dominance at the pet park or hormones making your dog behave aggressively.

Teaching Your Puppy to Play Gently

If you have ever watched puppies play with each other, you will notice that they correct each other if one becomes too rough. For example, a puppy may bite another puppy. The bitten pup will respond by yelping loudly and then refusing to play. This is called bite inhibition. The mother dog and your pup's littermates generally teach this, but the skill may need to be re-taught for interactions with humans. You may also find that your puppy did not yet master this skill when he came home to live with you. Fortunately, you can mimic the puppy behavior and teach this skill to your pet.

When your pup is too rough when playing, yell out Ouch loudly. Act as though your pup has seriously hurt you. Then, when he comes to see what is wrong, tries to comfort you, or tries to play, ignore your pup's attempts. Refuse to acknowledge him for a moment and then continue playing. If bite inhibition is an issue, you can allow your puppy to nibble on your hand. Say ouch and ignore him when he is too rough and then try again.

Encourage Gentle Interactions

It is common for excited puppies to want to bite or chew. This can be a problem in a home setting, especially with younger kids. To keep puppy from nibbling, offer him a chew toy before allowing your child to pet the pup. Then, scratch him behind the ears while your child pets. Young puppies do not have a long attention span, so keep these sessions short. Your puppy will be more likely to nip the longer he is being pet.

Taking Treats/Food Gently

Another way to teach your puppy restraint and how to be gentle is to teach the gentle command. This means to take the food or treat out of your hand nicely. Approach your dog and show him a treat. Then, close your hand on it. When your puppy nips at your hand, continue to keep it closed. If you do not want to or cannot tough out the pain from your pup's sharp teeth, wear a pair of gloves for this exercise. Eventually, your dog is going to realize that biting is not working and she will lick your hand or nibble very gently. Immediately open your hand completely and release the treat.

You should do this every time that you praise your dog with kibble or a treat. Let it be known that you will not give up the snack without gentle behavior.

Socializing with Other People, Pets, and Dogs

Once your puppy has had his or her shots and is ready to explore the world, you will want to start socializing them with others. You can set up play dates with other puppies for socialization or you can head over to the pet park to make friends with other dog owners.

As you socialize with others, the best thing you can do is pay close attention to your puppy's body language. It is very common for puppies to bark, growl, or lunge forward as they play, however, they will be in an uplifted mood when they do this. Watch for signs of aggression in your pup, such as yelping after being bitten, growling in a low, threatening pitch, or baring their teeth. You should also watch closely if a large and small dog breed are playing together, because small dogs are more likely to get hurt even when both pups are being friendly.

If your puppy does seem threatened or is becoming overwhelmed at any time, remove him or her for a time out. Let your puppy cool down for at least 5-10 minutes. If they will listen, tell them to lie down or sit for a while. This will help them relax a little, even if they do not realize they need to.

Interactions with humans and dogs outside of the home are important to your puppy's development. Regardless of whether your pup is inside or outside of the home, it is important that he acts with gentleness.

Chapter 7: Acceptance of Being Handled

Unlike gentleness, your puppy's mother does not teach acceptance of being handled. You will find, however, that it is essential to keeping your pup healthy and well groomed. When your pup does not accept that you are the leader and if you say he or she must be handled, you may find that they wiggle around too much when being groomed or visiting the veterinarian. When dealing with strangers, your puppy may even nip if they become frightened. To prevent this, you much teach your dog to accept being handled by yourself and strangers.

Teaching Your Puppy to be Handled

In the home environment, teaching puppy to be handled includes being friendly with children who may hug him or her and getting pup comfortable with basic grooming activities like brushing or bathing. You will also want to practice safety maneuvers like lifting, in case there is ever an emergency where you need to lift up your dog (regardless of its size).

Basic Handling Activities

Even if you choose to take your puppy to a groomer when he needs a bath or his nails trimmed, you will still find that there are times when you must handle your pup. Here are a few basic handling activities that you should work on at home, even if you plan on taking your puppy to a groomer to get his or her hygiene needs met.

Cleaning Gunk from Puppy's Eyes

Your veterinarian or groomer is not going to be there every time your puppy gets a gunked up eye, especially after sleeping. Use a moistened towel or tissue to clean sleepy goo out of the corner of your pup's eyes, as well as any goo leftover from an infection.

Brushing Puppy

You will find that even shorthaired breeds need a brushing from time to time. This is especially true if they play outside and get their fur filled with dirt and/or burrs. You will want to give your puppy a few brushes every day, even if they do not need it. This will get them used to the sensation.

Pick Through Your Pup's Coat

Even the best pet owners forget their pet's flea treatment from time to time. Since there is a chance you may have to pick fleas or even remove a tick from your pup, be sure to practice this. Pick through her coat as if you are looking for fleas. If you have ever seen a monkey pick for critters on another monkey's back, then you will do the same thing.

Lift Your Pup

Whether you are lifting you dog onto a table at the veterinary office or you need to lift your dog and save him in a life-threatening emergency, getting your puppy familiar with this sensation will make him more comfortable and less likely to resist. You may even find you need to lift large dogs from time to time, especially if they are in danger.

This is best practiced if you have already familiarized your dog with being restrained, since she will be more comfortable having your arms around her. Put your arms around either side of your puppy very briefly, rewarding with some kibble when you release her. Do this a few times, until your pup stays still for five seconds. The, lift her off the ground, gradually increasing the time that you hold her. If your puppy is small enough that she will likely be put on top of a veterinary or grooming table, you will eventually want to work up to placing your pup on the table and doing your handling exercises from the next section.

Teaching Your Puppy to be Restrained

Restraint is something that your pup should get used to, as you may need to restrain him for bath time or to meet new people. He may also be restrained at the veterinarian's or groomer's, especially if your pup is wiggly and will not sit still for his procedure.

Restraint should be taught at home, though it should be taught by hugging your puppy. Remember to move gradually. Additionally, if your puppy acts aggressively or wiggles too much, let go. Pressuring a puppy to be restrained outside of their comfort zone will cause them to relate a negative experience. This will make training the handling process a lot harder for you.

The best time to teach your puppy to be restrained is when he is relaxed and slightly sleepy. Start by picking your pup up by the scruff of its neck, as its mother would have after birth. In most cases, your pup will go completely limp. Place him in your lap and then loop one of your fingers through the collar and give pup kibble or a treat. You can also massage near your puppy's ears or on his chest to help calm him down. Once he is relaxed completely, turn your puppy over and rub his belly with a circular motion. Once pup is completely relaxed, practice picking him up, hugging him for a second, and then kissing him. Continue this exercise, gradually lengthening the amount of time that you hug (restrain) your puppy.

Once your puppy is completely comfortable with you hugging him, allow other members of your family to do the same exercise. Eventually, you will want to let your kids and even guests to your home hug your pup, to help him trust friends and strangers.

Teaching Your Pup to be Handled by Strangers

Your puppy will likely be handled by many strangers throughout life, as they visit the groomer, the veterinarian, or the dog kennel. If your pup is not used to being handled, you may find that they nip. Sometimes, your pup may be placed under anesthesia, restrained, or tranquilized if they will not behave or are considered a danger to the person handling them. This will result in a negative experience that will likely affect your pup's willingness to be handled in the future. To prevent this, it is important that you teach them to be handled by select strangers, particularly those that you leave him with.

Consider the way that your puppy may perceive being hugged vs. being restrained. Then, consider how your pup may perceive being handled vs. being examined. The behavior in each is almost the same; it is your puppy's perception that effects how they view the experience. If your pup is with someone that he loves and trusts, then he is likely to perceive that he is being handled and hugged. With a stranger, however, he is more likely to view it as being restrained and examined.

Getting Your Pup Used to Handling Sensations

The key to getting your pup used to being handled the way a groomer or vet will be handling her is providing the same sensations at home. This will prevent your puppy from becoming scared and lashing out at whoever is handling her. The sensations that you should replicate to familiarize your puppy with being handled for grooming or veterinary care will follow. As you practice these, do not move on to the next step before your puppy is completely comfortable with the step before it. Additionally, if you find that your dog tries to pull away from you or resists your behavior, keep your hands on him but follow instead of resisting. Imagine that your hands are stuck to puppy. Once he stops wiggling and lets you continue with handling him, you will reward with praise and/or a treat. The final thing you must remember is to perform handling exercises in a quiet, distraction-free environment several times each week to keep your dog comfortable with being handled.

#1: *The Collar*

Once you are in a quiet environment, touch your dog's collar, just beneath his chin. Grab quickly and then release him, praising each time. You should do this at least ten times to makes sure your dog is comfortable with it. Then, hold him for 2 seconds under the color before releasing. Continue to do this until your puppy allows you to hold his collar for ten seconds. Finally, hold your puppy under his chin and tug on the collar a little bit. If he does not resist, give him a treat. Once he is comfortable, move to the side and top of the collar, increasing both the duration and intensity for the remainder of practice.

#2: *Paws*

This is a sensitive area for pups, so you will likely find that your puppy is more resistant than he was with the collar training at first. Proceed very slowly, being sure that pup enjoys the exercise. You can trim your pup's nails to help with this exercise, though you should not do this unless you are certain on what you are doing. Dogs have veins that run into their nails, so cutting too much can cause pain and even make your dog bleed, even if you do not clip any skin. You should practice the below exercise with all of your puppy's paws with time. This exercise will likely take days before your pup is completely comfortable with it.

Start by picking up your puppy's paw and giving her some kibble. Do this five times, releasing immediately each time. Then, move up to holding your puppy's paw for one second after grabbing it. Slowly increase the time, according to how comfortable pup is. When she allows you to do this for a period of ten seconds, you will be able to move to the next step.

Now, you are going to work on moving your puppy's paw around. Hold it gently and move it a bit. When your pup is comfortable, massage the paws of her pad. Give her a treat. Then, press down on the pad to extend the toenails. Pretend to trim your pup's nails, if you are not comfortable doing it. If you are comfortable training her nails, clip one toenail each day and give your puppy a treat.

#3: Mouth

Start by touching your puppy's mouth and then giving her a treat with the other hand. Do this at least ten times. Then, slowly touch the puppy's mouth and pull up his lip so you can see one tooth. Give a treat if he allows you to do this. Continue to lift your pup's lips until more and more teeth are exposed. Do this on both sides of the mouth. Eventually, work your way up to opening the mouth. Give a treat.

Next, use a toothbrush to touch one of pup's teeth. Bruch one tooth and eventually work your way up to being able to brush pup's teeth as long as ten seconds without resistance.

#4: Ears

Stand in front of your puppy and reach around her head to touch her ear, giving a treat immediately after. When pup seems comfortable, hold her ear for one second. Release when she is still. If your puppy will not be still, stick to the puppy until you she does become still. Continue this until you dog is comfortable with you holding her ear for ten seconds.

Then, start massaging your pup's ear and manipulating it.

When she is comfortable, pretend that you are cleaning it (or actually clean it if you know what you are doing). The cleaning part of this is going to take several days or even longer if puppy is sensitive about her ears.

#5: Tail

Many dogs consider their tail to be private, so you may find puppy is sensitive about having his tail handled. Start slowly touching your pup's tail, giving a treat immediately afterward. Start to hold his tail, as he will let you, for one second at first and working your way up to ten seconds. When he allows you to do this, pull up on your dog's tail, brush it, and pull on it gently.

While you are exploring the tail area, you are also going to want to touch your dog's anus. Your veterinarian will regularly check his temperature and the sensitivity of this area can make your puppy have an aggressive response if he is not comfortable. After you lift the tail, use either a Q-tip or a gloved finger and just touch your puppy's anus. Continue to do this until puppy is comfortable for at least ten seconds, paying close attention to your pup's response and stopping as soon as he is uncomfortable.

Socialize Your Pup

Another important factor that determines how well your puppy will act when handled by strangers is how socialized they are. Puppies can be very social, trusting beings, but only if they are brought up that way. If you do not have other friends with dogs, consider going to a pet park to scout out friends for your puppy. Obedience school is another place your pup can make friends, though if you are training your puppy at home and do it properly, you may not need obedience school at all.

Establish Your Leadership

Like when you handle your pup yourself, you want to make it clear to your puppy that you are the leader and he or she must follow your direction. Having a strong bond with your pup will help, because it will make it clear that he or she can trust you. Additionally, your pup will know that when you leave them with someone (such as the veterinarian or groomer), you expect them to listen to that person. If your puppy respects your leadership, then they will trust your judgment.

By following the above tips, you will find your puppy ready and willing to be handled, whether it is by you, a veterinarian, a groomer, or someone else who may have close interaction with your pup. Remember to practice all of these regularly, because it is possible for dogs to become uncomfortable again. This is especially true with things that may scare them or involve sensitive areas, like handling the tail or lifting your pup. A quick refresher every few days will ensure that your puppy is susceptible to being handled his or her entire lifetime.

Chapter 8: Crate Training Your Pup

Dog crates often have a negative stigma surrounding them, especially since some dog owners leave their dogs in crates too much and negatively impact their health. When used properly, however, a crate is not a tool of cruelty. A crate is a safe place for your dog, where he or she will be able to escape when the house is too busy or they need to take a nap. Additionally, you will find it is incredibly useful for housebreaking, taking your pup to the vet, and other important doggie activities. Another benefit of crate training your dog is to reduce anxiety. Puppies (and dogs) instinctually feel that they must protect their home so if they see their crate as a home instead of the entire house, they will not feel obligated to protect such a large area. This chapter will teach you all you need to know about crate training your pup properly.

Choosing the Right Size Crate

There are good odds that you will need to buy more than one crate for your puppy in its lifetime. There are two reasons for this. First, your pup's crate must be large enough that it can stretch its legs and turn around. Your puppy should be able to stand up straight and be able to take a few steps comfortably. Second, your pup's crate must be small enough that there is not a lot of extra room. This is especially true when your dog is a puppy and not yet housebroken. Puppies have an instinct not to eliminate waste in their den, so this will help prevent accidents and make housebreaking easier.

If you do not want to buy two different crates for your puppy, you have two options. First, you can buy the right size crate to accommodate the size that you expect your puppy to grow to. To keep pup from using the bathroom in the crate, however, you will have to block a section of it off. A second option is to see if your local kennel or dog shelter rents out crates. If so, you can rent a crate for the duration of your pup's childhood and then buy only a larger crate once your pup ages.

Some Considerations Before You Start

Crating your dog is not necessarily a miracle intervention that makes them behave. If you do not approach it the right way, your puppy may become frustrated or feel trapped in the crate. This will lead to a negative experience that will make it very hard to crate train your pup.

#1: Time Your Pup's Crate Stays

Once your puppy is comfortable with the crate, you will want to be able to leave them in it to do things, such as go shopping or visit a friend. You may also have a job that you attend. If your puppy is under six months of age, you should not have him or her in the crate for more than 3 hours at a time. This is about how long young puppies can hold their bladder. Even adult dogs may need to go outside every three hours.

Additionally, you do not want to leave your puppy in her crate for long stretches during the day. This is especially true if your puppy sleeps in the crate at night. Crating your puppy for long periods can lead to health problems, including depression, anxiety, and even difficulties like arthritis from not being able to stretch her legs as much. If you cannot be there for your pup throughout the day, hire a pet sitter, switch up your work schedule, or find a puppy daycare.

#2: Do Not Make Negative Associations with the Crate

You should never call your puppy to the crate to punish him or her. Additionally, you should not lock pup inside as a form of punishment. The key to crate training your pup successfully, so they will not whine when shut inside, is making it a pleasant experience. Using it for punishment even once can lead to negative associations that deter your puppy from the crate, especially when they are young.

#3: Allow Your Puppy to Enter the Crate Voluntarily with Time

If you are training your puppy properly, there are good odds that you will eventually trust him enough to allow him free roam of the house unsupervised. This will likely happen as your pup enters adult hood and their age of mental maturity, usually around 12-18 months. Once your puppy does reach this stage, you should not shut him inside. Instead, allow him to go to his crate whenever he chooses to.

#4: Do Not be Overly Enthusiastic

Another essential key to successful crate training is to normalize the crate for your pup. This is especially true if you will be leaving him or her in their when you go to work or run errands. You can praise your puppy when he or she enters the crate voluntarily, but do this briefly. You should also ignore your puppy's excitement when you return home, letting pup out once he or she calms down.

Crate Training Your Puppy

Crate training is a process that may be more difficult for some puppies than others. In the beginning of your pup's life in your home, you may want to only keep pup in the crate overnight. It is highly likely that he will whine in the first couple nights- this is a normal reaction when your pup has been separated from his mom and littermates. If you cannot get puppy to like the crate enough that you can shut him in when you cannot supervise him, then consider using the leash method to keep your puppy in sight and out of trouble as you go through your daily routine in your house.

Step 1: Make the Crate Comfortable

To keep your puppy in the crate, he or she must feel comfortable in there. Line the floor of the crate with blankets and put 2-3 dog toys in there. Move the crate to an area where the family typically congregates, such as the living room.

As you are making the crate comfortable, you should also secure the door open in preparation for the next step. If the door swings shut or accidentally closes and hits your pup or traps him in, it is more likely that he will be scared of the crate.

Step 2: Casually Entice Pup Into the Den

The easiest way to get your puppy to enter the crate is to leave a trail of treats. Call your puppy to the room and lay down a few treats. Place a few more treats closer to the crate and then finally inside of it. Your puppy may or may not go all the way inside, but if they do not do so voluntarily then do not force them. If your puppy has a favorite toy, you can alternatively toss that inside of the crate to tempt them.

Step 3: Feed Your Pup Inside the Crate

Once your puppy has entered the crate voluntarily a few times, you will want to try feeding your puppy in the crate. If your pup seems reluctant, try feeding her nearby to create a positive association with the crate. Otherwise, place the food dish all the way at the back of the crate (you can start with it near the front and slowly move it farther back if you need to). Allow your puppy to eat and exit the crate.

Step 4: Distract Your Pup in the Crate

Another way to get your puppy comfortable enough to close the door is to distract him while inside the crate. Using a stuffed Kong toy or another distraction toy for puppies will keep your pup busy long enough to start familiarizing him with the crate. Place the toy toward the back of the crate and lure your puppy toward it using crates.

Step 5: Close the Crate

Once your puppy has gone into the crate a few times voluntarily to eat or chew on a distraction toy, you can start closing the door of the crate. Place your pup's food bowl inside. When she goes all the way in the crate, close the door. The first time, stand nearby and open the crate door as soon as she finishes eating. The next time, wait a few moments before opening the door. Prolong the time that pup is left inside after eating, adding a few minutes each time.

You may let your puppy out if she starts to whine. However, you must time this correctly. If you open the door as soon as she whines, she will not relate the two. If she finishes whining and then you open the door, she will relate whining with having the crate door opened. If this happens, keep pup in the crate until she stops whining.

Step 6: Familiarize Your Puppy with Staying in the Crate Alone

Once your puppy is comfortably able to withstand the crate for ten minutes when you are nearby, you will teach him to stay in it alone. Give your puppy food or a distraction toy and stand by for several minutes. Then, go into another room for several minutes. When you return, you will stay with pup for a few additional minutes before you let him out. It is important that he is calm when you let him out and not jumping and excited. If he is overly excited or whining, letting him out will teach him that whining or jumping is the way to get you to open the door. You will want to work up to at least 30 minutes of your puppy being alone before you can leave him home alone for long periods of time.

Step 7: Train Your Pup to Return to Her Crate on Command

Once your puppy is familiar with the crate, you will want to teach a command. Some good choices include go home or go to bed. The best way to train go home is by continuing to offer your puppy toys in the crate or feed her. Call your pup over to the cage. When she begins to enter, give her the command. Then, offer a treat or praise. Continue to do this until your puppy associates the command with going in the crate.

Once your puppy is crate trained, you will find that housebreaking is likely a breeze. The next chapter will teach you all you need to know about housebreaking with a crate, as well as other methods that you can use to potty train your puppy.

Chapter 9: Housebreaking Your Puppy

Housebreaking is something many pet owners dread, especially if they have had horror stories from other pet owners or have a preconceived stigma that housebreaking will be difficult. The good news is that it is actually quite easy to housebreak most puppies, especially since it is their instinctual nature not to use the bathroom where they live. This means that if you use the right technique the first time around, you will easily be able to housebreak your pup.

Essential Tips for Housebreaking Your Puppy

#1: Never Associate Negative Reactions with Pup's Natural Bodily Functions

A puppy that eliminates their waste in the house can be incredibly frustrating and it may be your first reaction to throw pup in his crate, yell at him, or rub his nose in it. If you do this, however, you will make your puppy feel bad about eliminating his waste at all. This will make him difficult to train, because he will associate bad reactions with his bodily functions, even if you praise him after he goes in the right area.

To correct your puppy for using the bathroom in the house, you must catch him in the act. If you do, quickly and calmly remove the puppy from the area and take him to the area where he is supposed to use the restroom.

#2: Know the Signs of Puppy Eliminating

A lot of keeping your house free of puppy's waste until he is housebroken is the responsibility of the owner. Most puppies can hold their waste for about 3 hours, so you should take your pup outside or to their bathroom area at least this frequently. Remember that younger puppies (4 months and below) often cannot control their muscles, so if you wait until they are exhibiting signs of using the restroom it may already be too late.

Once your puppy is a little bit older (and not yet housebroken), you can watch for signs that your pup has to use the bathroom. This could include circling, sniffing restlessness, or suddenly going to a quiet, discreet area to eliminate waste. If your pup understands which area he must use the restroom in, you may even find that he moves toward the door of your home. If your puppy is ready for housebreaking, you will find that he may bark, paw, or whine at the door to his bathroom area. If you notice any of these signs, act immediately to prevent pup from eliminating his waste in the house.

#3: Reward Pup for Going in the Appropriate Area

Once your puppy does go outside in the right area, give her a reward. As you praise pup, however, keep it short. You do not want to seem as if going to the bathroom outside is a big deal, since your puppy should view it as a normal activity. Quick and quiet approval or a small treat is enough to let your pup know that she has done a good job.

#4: Keep a Consistent Bathroom Area

You will want to take put to eliminate his waste in the same place every time. This is especially true in the early days of housebreaking. When you take your puppy to the same area, it will smell familiar and your puppy will eventually learn to recognize it and identify it with eliminating his waste. Additionally, try to take your puppy to the bathroom consistently at the same time.

#5: Regulate Puppy's Schedule to Predict When to Take Pup Out

If you feed your puppy at the same time each day, give a constant supply of fresh, clean water, and play with your puppy about the same amount of time, you will find that you can regulate your puppy's bathroom schedule. One thing that you will want to do is take your puppy to the bathroom as soon as you wake up, even before your coffee or brushing your teeth. You will find this is especially important in the early days of housebreaking when your pup is trying to associate the places, because he is almost guaranteed to go to the bathroom after being in his crate sleeping for several hours.

#6: Take Pup Outside 15-Minutes After Eating, Drinking, or Activities

While you should take your puppy outside every couple hours, you will also find that she is likely to want to eliminate waste approximately 15 minutes after she has been drinking, eating, playing, exercising, or being active. You will also find that your puppy generally has to go potty after waking up, but this should be done immediately.

#7: Do Not Get Frustrated if Pup Wakes You to Potty in the Middle of the Night

If your puppy wakes up in the middle of the night and needs to eliminate waste, he will likely whine to get your attention. While you do not necessarily want to get out of bed in the middle of the night, hide this disgruntled reaction from your pup. They will not need to use the potty in the middle of the night forever, but a negative reaction from you could put them off housebreaking for a while.

Another thing that you can do is pick up your puppy's water dish about 2 hours before bedtime. This will make it less likely they will need to go outside. Most pups are able to hold their bladder for 7 hours overnight using this trick.

#8: Clean Any Accidents Up Well

If an area smells like urine or feces, it is more likely your dog will use the bathroom in that area again. You want to clean anywhere that your pup has an accident extremely well to prevent future incidents. You also may want to consider investing in a cleaner made specifically for this purpose that is safe for use on carpets, as well as anywhere else puppy may have an accident.

Housebreaking Your Puppy

When you housebreak your puppy, you can do so using a crate and an outlet that leads to a small area for your dog to eliminate waste (called an exercise pen or ex-pen), install a doggy door that will lead to a safe potty yard for your dog to pee and poop in, housetrain using a crate, or teach your puppy to go in the litter box (if you have a small breed of dog).

Training with a Litter Box, Newspaper, or Puppy Pads

Unless you have a small breed that will use a litter box for its lifetime, these methods of training are not always successful. The reason for this is because these items are typically placed inside the house. Unless used with a crate that leads out to an exercise pen, you can confuse your pup into thinking it is okay to go in the house under certain circumstances. This has the potential of leading to accidents in the future.

For this method, you will combine the technique with either crate training or leash training. Simply follow the steps in the two sections below but instead of taking your puppy outside, remove him to the potty area.

Housebreaking Your Puppy with Crate Training

If you have already successfully crate trained your pup (as is likely because of your pup's age when she is ready to be housebroken), then you will find housetraining is a simple process. Any time you are unable to watch your puppy, you will place her in the crate. If you are watching her, be very aware of signs that she may need to use the bathroom. Take her outside (or to the designated restroom area) and then reward her when she goes.

Once your puppy is trusted not to go in her crate, allow her to be in one room of the house. You should slowly increase the amount of space/rooms that your puppy has access to, provided she is using the bathroom outside. If your pup does have an accident, take away the most recent space that has been given. Eventually, you will be able to allow your puppy in any areas of your home (provided she is well-behaved, of course).

Leash Training Your Puppy for Potty Training

The final option that you have for housebreaking is to leash train your pet. For this method, you are going to supervise your pup at all times. Put him on a leash and bring him with you as you do tasks throughout the day. When you need your hands free, tether him to something in the same room as you. As soon as you see your puppy showing signs of needing to eliminate (or if it has been a while since he has gone), use the leash to take him to the designated potty area.

If you are leash training your pup, you will find that it is very important to treat the yard (or other potty area) like any area of your home. Keep your pup on a leash as he does his business and then offer praise and a treat. Bring him inside on the leash as well. Once your puppy has been fully housebroken, you will be able to let him run around your house (and your yard if it is fenced in) without a leash.

Puppies are much easier to housetrain than older dogs, so you do have that in your favor! Otherwise, be patient with your puppy and pay close attention his or her needs to prevent accidents in the house. You will find that as with any part of training, consistency and disassociation with negative consequences are essential keys to properly housebreaking your puppy.

Chapter 10: Obedience Training

In this chapter, you will learn the best method to teach your pup each of the basic obedience commands, like come, heel, sit, lay down, and stay. If you want to train your pup other commands- do not worry- you will find a bonus chapter at the end of the book that teaches more advanced commands, tricks, and more. You will also find tips to help ensure your puppy listens every time you give him or her a command and not only when it is convenient for them.

Start by Teaching Your Puppy's Name

Before you start basic obedience training, it is important that you teach your puppy her name. Your puppy's name should always engage a positive reaction from you. For this reason, it is important that you do not discipline your puppy after saying his name.

The best way to teach pup's name is to use it frequently and positively. Always use an excited tone when you say your puppy's name. You may find that your pup associates this with come. You could choose to teach pup's name as an alternative to come, but other people find it is useful to keep the commands separate. This will eventually teach your puppy to look at you when you say her name.

General Tips for Obedience Training

#1: Keep Association with Your Puppy's Name Positive

To make training easier and encourage your dog to listen, you will want to call him or her by their name. Unfortunately, this will not necessarily work the way you would like it to if you call your puppy by his or her name and then punish them. When you are correcting your dog, avoid calling them by their name to prevent this negative association. This will grab your dog's attention and have them waiting for the positive reaction (or command) that will follow.

#2: Don't Associate Negative Interactions with Commands

It can be very tempting to tell your puppy to come when they have done something wrong or to tell them to go to bed so you can put them in time out. The problem with this, however, is that it associates negative occurrences with the commands you are giving. If you want your puppy to listen to your command every time, you must enforce it with positive rewards and plenty of praise.

#3: Change Your Words or Phrases if They Have Already Been Associated with Negative Cues

Sometimes, you accidentally associate a word with a negative consequence. Doing this just a handful of times can influence your training. If you make this mistake, choose a new word or phrase to use. For example, if you poison the word come, you could tell your puppy here instead. You will find that training your pup to come to a new word is much easier than disassociating the bad experiences of the previously used word.

#4: Choose High-Level Treats for Distracting Areas

As mentioned before, you will want to reward your puppy better when they perform well in a more distracting area. If you have already accomplished basic respect training, you can start to use treats to train your pup. Refer to Chapter 4 for tips on choosing the best hierarchy of treats for your puppy.

#5: Always Make Sure Your Puppy Eats and Uses the Restroom Before Training

The hardest thing to do is train your puppy when his or her instincts are telling them to do something else, like eliminate their waste or find something to eat. To have the most success with your training session, make sure these basic needs are met before you start training. This will help your puppy focus.

#6: Do Not Overwhelm Your Puppy

It can be very easy to get excited about teaching your pup a new command or trick. While it is good to be excited about training (because your puppy will get excited as well), it is important to remember that your puppy is young and does not have the patience or the attention span to focus on a task for a prolonged period of time. While you can train several times a day, you should not have training sessions longer than 15 minutes. You will also find that some dogs require even shorter training times before they become agitated, so follow your own instincts about what your puppy can handle.

#7: Don't Forget to Practice

Sometimes, we teach our puppies commands that we find we do not use very often. Even if you do not need to use the command, be sure to practice it regularly to keep your dog's mind and training sharp. Additionally, it ensures your puppy remembers what each command that he has been taught means.

Teaching the Come Command

Teaching your puppy to come when called is one of the basics of training your puppy. Additionally, you will find that this command could even save your pup's life one day. When taught correctly, your dog will come to you even when they are chasing a squirrel out into the street, avoiding a potentially deadly situation.

Step 1: Enlist a Helper and Play Ping Pong

The easiest way to teach commands is to make it fun. For this reason, have a friend or family member that your puppy with help you teach the come command. You will also need a tug toy and some tasty treats. Choose a distraction free area and sit down with your puppy, having your friend sit about 10 feet away. Hold your pup lightly and have the other person call your puppy with an excited tone of voice. Once puppy runs in that direction, give a treat and play tug-of-war. Do this a few times and then add the word you want to use, such as come or here when you call the dog. As your dog adjusts to this, you will want to move farther from your helper.

Step 2: Teach Your Dog Not to Pull Once Caught

Once your puppy has mastered coming when called, you are ready to teach a command such as gotcha. This phrase is one you will use once your dog has come and you have ahold of her collar and will deter her from pulling away. To teach this, show your dog a treat in your hand. Then, move away and hold the treat close to your body. Once your puppy comes to munch on the treat, hook your finger through the collar and say gotcha. Then, open your hand and give your pup the treat. As your puppy becomes more comfortable, grab her collar with your entire hand, more quickly than you did the first time. Continue to reward her for listening.

Step 3: Combining the Two

If your puppy has been successful at this training so far, the third and final step will be easy. Play ping-pong with your pup and a trusted friend again. This time, tell your dog to come and grab him, saying gotcha. When he holds still, respond with a treat.

Teaching the Heel Command

The Heel command is often used interchangeably with Let's go or Forward. This means that your pup will be walking on the left side of your body, keeping her head up and looking forward. You will be able to hold the leash loosely as your puppy walks and she will keep up with your pace. You can teach your puppy to heel inside the home or in a distraction-free area outside.

Step 1: Entice Your Pup with a Squeaky Toy

Hold your puppy's leash in your left hand (unless you want to train pup to heel to the right side) and hold the squeaky toy in your right. Position the toy by putting your arm across the front of your body and allowing it to hover just above and in front of your pup's head. Squeeze the toy a few times to grab his attention and then walk forward a few steps.

Step 2: Keep Puppy from Being Distracted

The reason you should train with a squeaky toy specifically is so you can grab your pup's attention. If you notice that she becomes distracted as you walk, squeeze the toy. This should focus her again and allow you to move forward.

Step 3: Offer Your Puppy Praise

Each time that your puppy starts moving forward again after you squeak the toy, praise him or give a treat. You can also praise him if he looks up at you for direction, which is called checking in.

Step 4: Keep Pup Focused for Longer Periods of Time

Once your puppy can focus on heeling at your side for at least 30 seconds at a time, you are going to want to slowly increase the attention your pup will give you. After a few minutes of exercises, stop and give your puppy some playtime. Eventually, move your training to the sidewalk or outside. Your puppy will heel every time you give the command in no time at all.

Teaching the Sit Command

There are two different ways that you can teach your puppy to sit. With both, you will need a treat and your hands to teach.

Method 1

Call your pup to you and praise him. Then, squat down next to him. Position one of your hands on his chest and the other hand behind his back legs. Command your puppy to sit, applying gentle pressure against the backs of his knees and a gentle upward pressure on his chest. Guide your pup down into a seated position and reward him with a treat and plenty of praise immediately.

Method 2

This method requires you to use a puppy treat as a lure. Position the treat in front of your puppy's nose, but not so close that she can snap at it. Tell puppy to sit, as you move the treat higher in the air. Her nose should follow so she can nibble at the treat and naturally, her bottom will move downward. If she backs up or puppy does not sit, use your free hand to apply pressure to your puppy's backside and guide her to a seated position. Once again, give a treat and praise as soon as pup is seated.

Teaching the Lay Down Command

This command may be hard to teach. This is especially true if you have a shy puppy or a puppy that is always moving. Stay patient and continue to practice and eventually your pup will grasp the concept. There are two methods that you can use to teach the lay down command, depending on the likelihood of your puppy moving around.

Method 1

Start by giving your puppy the sit command. Then, kneel down beside him. Place your right hand behind your puppy's front legs and your left hand behind his shoulders. Issue the down command and scoop your pup's legs out gently while pressing on the shoulder area until he is in a laying position. Pet the length of his back to help pup relax and then give him a treat.

Release your pup using a chosen release word like okay. Practice this having him lay down for lengthening periods of time. Eventually, you will find your puppy lies down without the guidance of your hands.

Method 2

If your pup is highly anxious or is too excited to lie down, the following method may work better.

Start as you did in the previous method, kneeling down beside your pup as she sits. This time, hold a treat in front of his face with your right hand and place your left hand on her shoulders. Issue the down command and bring the treat toward the floor, in between your puppy's paws. Then, move the treat straight out across the floor, as if you are making an 'L' shape. Once your puppy has achieved a laying position, give her a treat.

Teaching the Stay Command

For this command, it is important that your puppy is already familiar with sit and does so when you tell him to.

Step 1: Put Your Pup on the Leash and Have Her Sit

Start by attaching your puppy to a leash. Position her so that she is on the right side of your body and give the sit command. When she is seated, move on to the next step.

Step 2: Position Yourself and Give the Stay Command

Now, turn your body so that you are facing your pup and hold your hand near his face, giving the command to Stay. Take two steps backward, keeping the leash slack. After a few seconds, walk back to where you were standing by your dog and tighten the leash, holding it down so it is not tight but also so that your puppy cannot jump up.

Step 3: Release Pup

Once your puppy stays still through this for a few moments, say a release word like okay, preferably the same word you used when teaching your pup to lie down. Then, give your puppy a treat to reinforce the good behavior. Eventually, you will be able to have him stay for longer periods of time.

If your puppy gets up after being told to stay, have pup sit down. Once he is sitting, return to your position in front of him and repeats the stay command with the hand signal.

These five commands are the most essential and they fall under those that every well-trained dog should know. Beyond this, however, there are more commands and even tricks that you can teach your puppy. If you want to advance your puppy's obedience training beyond the basics, be sure to check out Chapter 12.

Chapter 11: Correcting Your Pup for Unwanted Behaviors

While you can do your best to give your puppy all of the attention and training that he needs in the first few months that he lives in your home to thrive, sometimes, puppies do still develop behavioral problems. Fortunately, with the right preventative measures and by addressing puppy problems immediately and not just letting them slide, you can help stop behavioral problems before they become severe issues.

Prevent Jumping

Often, puppies jump up when they are trying to get attention. If you acknowledge your pup, even by pushing her away or bringing your knee up to her chest, you are giving her that attention. Your pup will not be deterred by the negative attention at all, because she is still getting what she wants.

Instead, deter your puppy by giving her no attention. Turn away from her and firmly say no with your arms crossed.

Ignore your pup, even if you have to go in another room. When she has all feet on the ground, praise her with petting and attention. If she knows the sit command, you can also tell her to sit and give a treat. If your dog continues to jump when you turn around, repeat the above practice until you have instilled it that you will not give your dog the attention she wants from jumping.

Stopping Mouthing, Biting, and Nipping

Puppies cannot explore the world around them with hands as humans can. For this reason, they often use their mouths to feel, mouth, or even bite things that they can reach- from inanimate objects they may chew on to human body parts that come close to their face. Even though you may be tempted to let this seemingly cute puppy behavior slide, make sure to break it immediately because destructive chewing and biting are two bad behaviors that may result.

Step 1: Teach Pup that Human Skin is Sensitive Using Bite Inhibition

Eventually, you will teach your puppy that human skin should not be touched at all. First, however, you should teach the appropriate gentleness of teeth on human skin. This is a technique called bite inhibition. If your puppy is not already familiar with it, you can find instructions for bite inhibition in Chapter 6.

Step 2: Follow These Tips to Stop Pup from Putting His Mouth on Human Skin

There are several things that you can do to help prevent your pup from mouthing your skin in the first place. Check out these tips to deter this type of behavior.

#1: Play without Contact

It can be incredibly tempting to rough house with your puppy or wrestle with her. If you do this, however, you make it more likely that your puppy will get in the habit of nibbling on your skin. Instead, use tug toys and other ways of playing with your pup in a no-contact way.

#2: Substitute for Human Flesh

When your puppy nibbles, give him a bone or a chew toy. This is especially beneficial for nibbling on fingers and toes. Additionally, during times that your pup is likely to chew on you (like if you are holding or petting him), use small treats to distract him or some kibble. This will teach him to enjoy being touched without the need to nibble whoever is petting him.

#3: Prepare for Ambushes

It is not uncommon for puppies to come charging at you when you walk, ready to play and nip at your ankles. If this seems to be a problem for your pup, get in the habit of keeping kibble or a toy in your pocket. When he ambushes you, stop moving and tempt him with the toy or kibble instead. If you do not have the kibble or the toy handy, stop moving until your puppy stops, letting him know that you are not going to engage with his chewing behavior.

#4: Keep Your Puppy Interested in Her Toys

One reason that your pup may stray from her toys and nibble on you instead is because she is bored. Regularly provide new entertaining toys for your puppy. Use caution not to give her too many, however, or you may find that she hides them around the house as a show of dominance.

#5: Have Puppy Play Time

Another way to keep your puppy interested in playtime is to involve her with other dogs (who have been vaccinated and are well-behaved, of course!). Playing with other dogs (especially older dogs) and having the chance to socialize will improve your puppy's development. It will also teach her new behaviors (this can be a good or bad thing, so pick playmates carefully!) and help release some of the energy and desire that she has to play rough.

Step 3: Advanced Tips for Puppy's Mouthing Behavior

Sometimes, even when you do all of the tips from Step 2, puppy may still have the desire to gnaw on you. In this instance, there are two different methods you can use to deter pup.

Method 1

Pick up a non-toxic spray deterrent from your local pet supply store that is made to deter your puppy from chewing. Spray this to areas of your skin that your pup frequents to chew. Then, when he does try to chew this area, he will have a bitter taste in his mouth that makes him want to let go. As soon as your puppy does let go of your skin or clothing, give him plenty of praise. You should not have to use this technique for more than 2 weeks before pup learns his lesson.

Method 2

In this method, you will give your puppy a time out for biting. You should note that you should never give your puppy a time out in his crate, because his crate is supposed to be his safe place and not an area of punishment.

When you feel your puppy's mouth on your skin (even the slightest amount) you are going to yelp loudly as you did when teaching bite inhibition. Then, walk away from the area and ignore your pup for at least 30 seconds. If he tries to bite or follows you, leave pup in the room (if it is puppy-proof). Return calmly after 30 seconds and continue the activity you were doing when pup put his mouth on you.

Step 4: Be Wary of Signs of Aggression

In some cases, your yelping and time-outs may cause your puppy to lash out aggressively. Pay close attention to your pup's body language and watch out for hard biting out of what seems to be fear or anger. You can help prevent this by developing a strong bond with your puppy, keeping your fingers and other body parts away from her face, and refraining from smacking pup when she bites. Additionally, be sure to still continue playing with your puppy, just be sure to do so in a way that involves toys instead of wrestling or rough housing with her.

How to Stop Destructive Chewing

When puppy chews up a shoe, a remote, or a kid's toy that she is not supposed to, it can be incredibly frustrating. Some of your puppy's chewing can even be dangerous, especially if she has access to chemicals, toxic plants, or sharp bits of plastic or metal. With the right steps, however, you can take the necessary precautions to prevent your puppy from chewing. This section will discuss these steps, as well as what you can do if your mischievous pup starts to develop a chewing habit.

Step 1: Have a Test Done to Check for Nutritional Deficiencies

Sometimes, puppies chew as an effect of a disease called pica. This causes dogs to chew on things, particularly those that contain the nutrient or mineral they may be missing. There are also other conditions that may cause a dog to chew. In most cases, a simple blood test at your local veterinary office can help you rule out nutritional deficiencies and your veterinarian will know what other signs to check for in your pup.

Step 2: Make Your Home Puppy Proof

The best way to deter chewing is to puppy proof your home and to look around a room before you leave pup alone in it. While you may think puppies will only chew on shoes, cords, and similar items, you also must be cautious of cell phones and electronics, remotes, and anything else that pup may want to explore.

As you puppy proof your home, do not only focus on the things that puppy may chew up. Also, be cautious of bottles of dangerous chemicals, poisonous plants, and other items that may harm or even kill your pup if chewed on.

Step 3: Give Your Puppy Plenty of Acceptable Chewing Items

One of the best ways to deter pup from chewing is to give him toys of his own. Some good options include dog toys and chew sticks. Some dogs also like bones, though you must be very cautious since dogs with larger teeth may break off small, sharp, dangerous pieces that could be swallowed. Rawhide and beef bones are generally preferred and you should never give your puppy chicken bones, because they splinter and have the potential to puncture your pup's digestive tract. Additionally, do not give your puppy something that resembles a no-chewing item, like an old pair of shoes. This will confuse your pup and possible lead to him chewing on the wrong pair of shoes.

Step 4: Correcting Your Puppy for Inappropriate Chewing

If you do catch puppy in the act of chewing (remember not to punish her if you catch her after the item has already been chewed), you can scold her. Take the item and firmly tell her no. Then, take pup over to her toy area and give her something that is acceptable to chew on. When your puppy begins to gnaw at the bone or toy, give her plenty of praise.

How to Stop Excessive Barking

In most cases, your puppy will bark when he has a need that must be fulfilled. This does not mean, however, that you should let bad behavior continue. You must remember that when your puppy barks, it is likely to get your attention. For this reason, you should not yell at your dog or scold him for his behavior.

Step 1: Do Not Acknowledge the Barking

Face it. When you come home and your cute ball of fluff is jumping around and so excited to see you, your first reaction is to greet your friend. This, however, will become a costly mistake because it trains your puppy to bark when he is excited and that it is okay to bark to get your attention. For this reason, it is critical that you do not acknowledge your pup's barking. If simply ignoring your pup is not an option, turn around or go to another room until he calms down.

Step 2: Reward Your Puppy When She is Calm

Once your puppy has calmed down, reward her with plenty of praise and your attention. You should do this immediately to ensure your pup makes the connection between calm interaction and praise. If your puppy starts to bark once you give her attention, ignore her again and follow with praise once she is calm.

Step 3: Keep Your Pup Active and Disciplined

Sometimes, your puppy may bark at you because they are not stimulated enough. Puppies are not creatures that will keep themselves entertained for long periods of time. They require plenty of stimulation and discipline to develop into a well-rounded dog. To keep your pup busy and provide that much needed stimulation, give him or her plenty of exercise. You should also give your pup enough toys to play with, walk pup often, and keep him or her busy with command training on a regular basis throughout the day.

How to Stop your Puppy from Digging

When your puppy digs, they are acting on instinctual behavior, often as a means to solve their boredom. It can be hard to prevent your pup from digging, but you will do so by redirecting their attention.

Step 1: Do Your Research

Digging is an instinctual behavior that can be found in all dogs' ancestry lines. The reason that puppies dig when they are bored is because they are trying to exert energy. Some puppies are more notorious for needing to dig than others, so do your research to find out if your puppy is highly susceptible to this behavior. Additionally, research how much active play your breed needs and adjust that amount to meet your pup's needs.

Step 2: Correct Your Puppy

If you do catch your pup in the act of digging, sternly tell him no. Then, redirect his energy to active play, like playing fetch (you can learn how to teach this in the next chapter) or a game of tug. Once your puppy is running around or playing in an appropriate way, reward him with praise.

Step 3: Provide More Energy-Reducing Play for Your Pup

If you notice that your puppy is digging despite your best efforts, it is possible that your puppy is not getting enough physical activity for their specific breed. One way to increase the energy that your pup expels during playtime is to buy a backpack for your puppy to wear while you play for 30 minutes. This will make your pup expel as much energy as they would in a full hour of play.

How to Stop Excessive Urination

When your puppy urinates for a reason other than to go to the bathroom, it is often because he is either excited or intimidated. Read on to learn a technique to deal with each of these problems.

Excited Urination

The good news is that excited urination is usually considered a puppy behavior that will cease once your puppy gains control of his or her bladder. Regardless, excited urination is most likely to happen when your pup has a full bladder. Take your puppy for frequent trips to the bathroom to prevent the likelihood of excited urination.

Submissive Urination

When a puppy is intimidated or afraid, it can sometimes cause what is known as submissive urination. This will need training to prevent the behavior. In most cases, you should start by considering your own body language. Dogs are very in-tune to body language and if you are giving off an angry or scary demeanor, then it can trigger the submissive urination.

When you respond to submissive urination, it is important that you do not cause additional fear or anxiety in your pup. Speak in a calm voice and be very cautious of your own body language. Remove your puppy to the appropriate urination area and praise him when he uses the bathroom, as you would while housebreaking pup. If you find that it is new situations or encounters causing your pup distress, try introducing them more slowly to help pup familiarize and relax.

Curbing Aggressive Behavior

It is highly unlikely that puppies will develop aggressive behavior, unless they experienced a violent or scary home environment during the first couple months that they were living with their mother. The good news is that you can likely curb aggressive behavior by teaching your puppy bite inhibition and how to be gentle, in addition to making sure they have enough socialization with people and animals outside of your home. If you taught these techniques and your pup still shows aggression, use the following technique.

Step 1: Anticipating and Preventing an Attack

If you notice your puppy behaving aggressively toward you, the first thing that you must do is take the necessary steps to prevent an attack. Some common signs of aggression include bearing of the teeth, raised hair, or a low, menacing sounding growl. The first thing that you must do is to remain calm, but assertive. Turn your body so that it is slightly to the side, avoiding making eye contact with your puppy (dogs often see eye contact as a challenge). Very calmly, own your space. Show your puppy that the space you are in is your own and that you will respect pup's space as well. Take a step forward and own your space. If you have an umbrella or purse handy, you can set this down in front of you as a means of claiming your space.

In most cases, you can avert a dog attack by remaining calm and assertive and putting up an invisible barrier between you and your puppy. This will let the pup know there is no threat. If your dog attacks despite your actions, however, you will move to the next step.

Step 2: What to Do If Your Puppy Attacks

If your puppy still moves forward to attack, the best thing you can do is distract your puppy while you move to safety. If you are wearing a sweater or carrying something, wave it in your pup's face and try to get him to direct aggression toward that item. If this does not work, protect your throat, face, and chest. Keep your fists balled to prevent pup from biting your fingers. If you cannot avoid being bitten, try to direct the bite to your shin or forearm, as these are the safest and least likely to cause fatal damage. If you can, get your pup into a submissive position or forcefully remove him to his cage.

Keeping yourself safe in this situation is critical.

If your puppy does attack, he may not again for a while. You should consult with a behavioral specialist and carefully monitor interactions between yourself and your puppy in the future. Send pup for a time out at the first signs of agitation or aggression.

Step 3: Safety First- Preserving the Safety of Other People and Animals

If you have identified signs of aggression in your puppy, you should not have her around other people or animals until the aggression is handled. If your puppy attacks or bites you, there is a much higher likelihood that they will do this to another animal or even a person walking by your house. Do not leave your puppy outside unsupervised, even in a fenced in area. Additionally, always have your puppy on a leash in areas where there are other people or animals. Authorities have been known to order dogs to be euthanized for this type of behavior, so it is important to prevent your puppy from lashing out at others.

Stopping Your Pup's Separation Anxiety

Have you ever left the house (or the room, in some cases) and had your puppy pee on things, chew up what she could reach, or whine incessantly? If so, it is possible that your puppy is dealing with a case of separation anxiety, which is distress experienced by your puppy whenever you leave. This section will teach you how to deal with this behavior.

Diagnosing: Separation Anxiety or Simulated Separation Anxiety?

You will notice a number of symptoms if your dog has separation anxiety, including whining, barking, excessive salivation, scratching doors, walls, carpets, and floors, destruction of properties, or attempts to escape the area he is confined to. If these symptoms present in your puppy, there are one of two possible causes. The first is separation anxiety, which causes an incredible amount of stress in your pet that causes him to behave this way.

The second possible cause of these symptoms is simulated separation anxiety, which is caused when you react to the mess he has caused on a previous occasion. He now acts out when you leave because he knows he will receive attention (even if it is negative) for his behaviors.

Handling Simulated Separation Anxiety

Simulated separation anxiety is not too difficult to deal with. The first thing that you can do is crate your puppy whenever he cannot be supervised. You should also gradually increase the amount of time pup spends in there to get him used to it. Finally, be sure to consistently train your puppy to be obedient, give him enough exercise, and exhibit strong leadership that your puppy looks up to.

Handling Actual Separation Anxiety

Separation anxiety is an actual medical problem that dogs can develop. Puppies look up to us as a pack leader and when we take them places with us, as we must in their earlier puppy days, they get accustomed to this. When they are left alone from time to time, as they are older and able to be trusted, this change in routine, paired with your absence, can cause separation anxiety.

Medication

In some cases, a puppy's separation anxiety is so stressful that their veterinarian may prescribe something to help the pup relax when their owner is home. You should know that this is not a permanent solution for your puppy's separation anxiety and this should only be administered when necessary, up until you have appropriately dealt with your puppy's separation anxiety problem.

Training Your Puppy to Be Alone

Obedience training is something that must happen continually for your pet. After you have taught him basic commands, teach your puppy what is expected of him. Have him sit or lie down in a room and then leave. Praise him if he is still lying when you return. Teach your puppy to enjoy his crate and also that you will always return. Imbed the training of your puppy to be alone into his other obedience training as you teach your pup how to behave. When he is behaving appropriately, provide plenty of affection to reinforce good behaviors in your puppy so he continues to repeat these actions.

Preventing Boredom

Another essential part of keeping your puppy's separation anxiety from flaring up is to prevent boredom. If you leave your pup alone in a room or her crate, make sure she has toys and things to chew on if she would like. A stuffed Kong toy is also a good option for your pup, since it will keep her busy for a while. You should also be sure to keep plenty of time for activity and walking in your pup's schedule. Finally, take your puppy on a walk or have playtime just before you leave your puppy alone to help her release pent-up energy.

How to Stop Obsessive Dog Behavior

The reason that obsessive dog behaviors are dangerous is because it can cause puppy to play more intensely at some times than others, during which she may become over excited or even aggressive. This obsession is often tied to a specific toy, object, or game.

Step 1: Identifying the Behavior

It is very easy to identify when your dog has entered the zone of obsession. You will see that your dog is not enjoying playtime. Rather, your dog will be playing the game or chewing on the object as if he is in a trance. This trance-like state will appear as a staring, blank appearance and a fixated, determined interaction, but without any joy.

Step 2: Gauge Your Puppy's Enjoyment While Playing

One of the best ways to prevent obsessive behavior is to stop it before it starts. Only you know your puppy, so as you learn how your pup typically acts during play you can curb her behavior when it becomes too intense. This will teach your puppy that you control how intensely she may play and that there is an acceptable level of playing and an unacceptable level.

Step 3: Withdraw Your Pup When Play is Too Intense

Consider your puppy's levels of play, from a 1 of barely interested to a 10 of obsessive play. Once you know what your puppy's level 10 is, you should withdraw pup from play just before he reaches that level. You can have him lie down for quiet time, go to his crate and relax for a while, or redirect his attention to a different toy or method of play.

Step 4: Give Your Puppy Plenty of Outlets

Often, puppies behave with obsessive behavior because they are using it as an outlet for energy or anxiety. To help prevent this, make sure your pup has plenty of toys to keep him busy. You should also go on several walks, allow plenty of playtime with other people and dogs, and provide mental stimulation through obedience training.

How to Stop Hyperactive Puppy Behavior

In many cases, a hyperactive pup is behaving in this manner because they are not being stimulated enough in their current environment. This can leave them with pent-up energy that they need to expel. This section will teach you a few techniques that you can use to help curb hyperactive puppy behavior.

Step 1: Ignore Your Pup's Behavior

In some cases, your puppy will jump around or act excited to get your attention. Even though this is cute, acknowledging your pup's behavior teaches him that acting out will get him the attention he wants (even if it is negative). The best thing that you can do is to ignore your puppy's bad behavior. Do not touch him, do not make eye contact, and refrain from talking to your pup. Leave the room if you must, but do not acknowledge the bad behavior at all. Once your puppy calms down, you can then reward him with your attention.

Step 2: Redirect Your Puppy's Energy

Once you have successfully ignored your puppy's bad behavior and rewarded them for calming down, you should redirect your pup's energy to another activity. There are a few different ways you can achieve this. First, you can give your puppy a specific job to do. An example of this would be strapping a book bag to your dog so he carries while you walk. This redirects energy and his attention away from bad behaviors, like chasing squirrels or other critters. Another option is to take your puppy for a walk so he can expel some of the energy that is causing hyperactivity.

Step 3: Consider Your Role in Your Puppy's Hyperactivity

As the pack leader, your puppy will often look to you for guidance and direction. When you are in a heightened state of energy, you may find that your puppy mirrors the way that you feel. Are you thinking stressful thoughts or anxious about something? If so, this may communicate through your facial expressions, body language, and tone of voice. Be cautious of these as you interact with your puppy and try to feel calm instead.

Step 4: Consider Aromatherapy

There is a reason that so many baby lotions are infused with lavender; it's because aromatic lavender produces a calming effect on the body and mind. Aromatherapy could benefit anxious pups in the same way, whether you infuse the oils and release them in the air or use another means of aromatherapy. This method is especially suitable for dog breeds that are incredibly hyperactive naturally. Speak to your veterinarian about the best calming oils for aromatherapy, the appropriate dosage, and how you should administer them to your puppy.

How to Stop Your Puppy from Being Distracted on Walks

Sometimes, even puppies that have been successfully taught to walk on a leash and follow commands like heel can become distracted. This is especially true as they are enticed by the familiar smells of the neighborhood around them. Puppies often pull on their leash or stop and sniff familiar smells, which makes for a long and aggravating walk.

The easiest way to train your puppy to walk when you tell him to is to entice him with a treat. When he is distracted, get a high-value treat and put it slightly in front of your puppy's nose, just enough that he is able to catch a whiff of it. Walk away from the distraction and your pup should follow, in pursuit of the enticing treat. Give the puppy the treat after 15 feet of walking. Continue to do this when your puppy gets distracted, being sure to lengthen the amount your pup is walking each time. Eventually, you will only give a treat once the entire walk has been completed.

How to Curb Persistent Fear and Anxiety

Even the biggest of dogs may run and hide when a violent storm is passing overhead. When your puppy seems to be afraid of everything, however, it can make it very difficult to enjoy life with your pup. This is especially true if she spends more time cowering than she does playing.

The most common cause of persistent fear and anxiety in puppies is a lack of self-confidence. Overcoming this is possible, though it will be a long road of building your puppy's self-esteem. It is challenging but will be well worth it once your puppy no longer cowers when the kids are blowing bubbles.

How to Build Your Puppy's Self-Esteem

Build self-confidence is a long one, since it is a mental change that your puppy must go through. The easiest way to accomplish this in a dog is to help your puppy achieve goals. Whether it is completing a small obstacle course or going outside to use the bathroom alone, help your dog accomplish goals and then offer praise to celebrate. Your dog will learn to feel good when he accomplishes things and it will boost his self esteem as a result.

It is not uncommon for even the best trained puppies to

develop behavioral problems from time to time. Fortunately, if you have an understanding of the underlying cause of the behavior and a good way to handle it, you can overcome almost any mischievous puppy behaviors.

Chapter 12: Advanced Obedience Training

This chapter is included to teach your puppy more than just the basics. While the five commands discussed in Chapter 10 are the only essential commands, you will find that many of the commands included in this chapter make communicating with your pup earlier. Better communication, in turn, will lead to a more obedient pup that behaves in the manner that is expected of him in your home.

Stand

Teaching your puppy stand is rather simple.

Step 1: Entice Pup with a Treat

Start by having your dog get into the seated position using the sit command. Entice him with a treat and then hold it about six inches from his face.

Step 2: Giving the Command and Moving the Treat

Give the command stand and move the treat away from your dog's face, keeping it at the same level as his nose. He will have to stand to reach the treat and when he does, you will reward him. You will practice this until your puppy stands without you guiding him with a treat.

Training Your Pup to Ask to Go Outside

By the time puppies have reached adult age, they are most likely housebroken. You may find that they paw at the door or stare at you or bark and run around when they need to go outside to relieve themselves. However, some owners still seem oblivious to this (particularly a spouse who has had a long day at work and is zoned out in the television or kids that do not pay attention to these signs). In this case, you may find that it is helpful to teach your pup to ask to go outside.

Step 1: Associate Bell Ringing with Going Potty

The easiest way to do this is to attach a wind chime or a sleigh bell to the door of your home. Each time that you take the puppy outside, ring the bells on your way out.

Step 2: Reward Pup's Curiosity in the Bell

Eventually, your pup is going to become curious and sniff the bells to see what they are. Praise him with good boy or yes when he does this, repeating this each time that he is interested in the bells. Your puppy will soon start to associate the bells with going to the bathroom.

Step 3: Getting Pup to Ring the Bell

When your puppy does make the correlation and rings the bells for himself the first time, give him praise and a treat. Give him more treats if he does use the bathroom, to strengthen the connection.

Go To "Place"

There are times when you will want to send your puppy to a certain area. For example, you may send him to the living room if someone is at the door or you may want to have him sit by the door to be introduced to guests. You may also find that there are times when you want your furry friend to go lie in his crate or bed for a while.

Step 1: Put Your Puppy on the Leash

You can use the go to "place" command for any area that you send your puppy and the technique to teach it will be the same. Start by putting your puppy on a leash and say the cue word, such as "bed" or "living room" or "door".

Step 2: Lead Puppy to the Area and Treat

Take your puppy to the place where you want her to go and give a treat as soon as you get there. Continue to practice this until your puppy goes to the place after your command.

Step 3: Have Pup Lay Down and Stay in the Area

Once he does, begin to give the command to lie down and stay. Have your dog lie down for at least 15 seconds and give her the cue to get up and a treat. Continue to practice this until your puppy can stay in place for at least three minutes.

Sit on the Street Corner

Puppies just don't seem to grasp that streets are a dangerous place, even as cars zoom by. Additionally, it is nearly impossible to teach this correlation without letting your pup get hurt. For this reason, it can be incredibly useful (and even life-saving) to teach your puppy to sit on the corner of the street. You will want to teach your dog to sit before teaching this command.

Step 1: Take Pup for a Walk

Start by taking your puppy out for a walk. When you get close to the street corner, have pup heel so that she is walking close to you.

Step 2: Have Pup Sit on the Corner

When you reach the corner, give the command to sit. If puppy knows this command, you should have no problems.

Step 3: Reward Your Puppy

Once pup is sitting, give her a reward. You should do this every time that you walk her. This will relate the act of sitting on the corner to getting a treat, which will be incredibly helpful if she ever gets away from you while walking.

Shake (Body)

This command should not be confused with shake (hands). In this instance, the owner often gives the shake command so the dog dries off after swimming or being bathed so they do not soak the towel (or their owner). You can also teach shake head, shake tail, and similar commands using this technique.

Step 1: Getting Your Puppy to Shake

The good news is that this command is relatively easy to teach, since most dogs will instinctually shake their body after getting their fur wet to dry off. You will give the shake command as your dog is already shaking off after getting their fur, giving plenty of phrase afterwards and getting excited.

Step 2: Learning the Command

Eventually, they will relate the command shake to the motion and you can give the command when they are outside rolling around and need to come in or when their fur is full of bits of dirt and grass.

Stop

Stop is a useful command, particularly if it is taught as a way to make your dog discontinue whatever behavior she is currently engaging in. This can help if she is chewing something she is not allowed to, if she is venturing too far outside, to signify to stop barking, or for any other adverse behavior.

Step 1: Catch Pup in the Act

If you remember from the previous chapter on correcting bad behavior, then you know that you should not yell at your puppy when they are caught in the act. In most cases, you were instructed to remove the puppy from the problem and redirect their energy somewhere else.

Step 2: Correct Pup

You will teach your puppy the stop command in the same scenario. When you remove your pup from the offending situation, you will calmly and firmly say stop.

Step 3: Redirect Puppy's Focus and Give Praise

Then, you will redirect her behavior and give her praise. With time and use in many situations, you will find that your pup starts to relate stop with ceasing whatever displeasing behavior she is currently engaged in.

Touch

The cue to touch something (with your dog's nose) is one that is useful for two different reasons. First, if you would like to have your puppy go somewhere (such as the left or right side of your body), you will use this cue to move him without using physical force. The second reason you may use this cue is to train your puppy to participate in obstacle courses or sports. Often, you will find that your pup is required to touch his nose to a particular area to play in the race or to earn extra points.

Step 1: Tempt Pup

Take a moist treat and rub it across your palm, being sure to layer enough on so that your hand smells like the treat.

Step 2: Get Pup to Touch Your Hand and Praise

Then, put your hand out so it is 12 inches from your pup's nose. Hold out your palm and say touch. The smell should lure him in to touch his nose to your palm. If he does, give him a treat and praise.

Step 3: Troubleshooting the Technique

If you find that your puppy is reluctant to touch your open hand (as may happen if your dog is trained to be gentle), you can teach this skill using your closed fist instead of your palm.

Back Up

Back up is a useful command that instructs your puppy to take a few steps back. You will need to know stay for this command if you do not want training to be difficult. It can be used toward objects, like if your puppy is standing too close to a door, or when your puppy is approaching people, especially those that may not be comfortable with your pup yet.

Step 1: Have Your Puppy Stay

Start by having your puppy stay. Walk a few feet in front of her, putting your hand out and turning so you face your pup.

Step 2: Get Your Pup to Back Up

Start to move forward toward your puppy, hand still out. In most cases, a dog will instinctually back up as you walk toward them. If your puppy does not back up, lean your body forward as you walk toward her. Give pup praise and a treat.

Step 3: Troubleshooting the Technique

If you cannot get your puppy to back up at all, use your leg to gently nudge your dog backwards when you reach her. Give praise and a treat as soon as she starts to back up.

Step 4: Teach the Back Up Command

Once your puppy has done this a few times and seems to understand what you expect, start to use the back up command. Tell your puppy to back up as you move forward and reward with a treat.

Drop It

This command can be used in two different instances. First, it can be given when your puppy picks up something that she is not allowed to have from the floor. It can also be used for toys, if you are playing fetch with your puppy. Remember never to use it to take a toy away for punishment, however, because that can create a negative association with the command.

Step 1: Gather Some Things Pup Cannot Chew

To teach a pup to drop it, get some chewable items (like an old shoe or a kid's toy) and some mid-to-high value treats. Take one of the items and tempt your puppy.

Step 2: Get Pup to Drop the Item

As he puts his mouth on the item, say drop it as you bring a treat to your pup's nose. Your puppy will likely open his mouth to take the treat.

Step 3: Reward for Dropping the Item

Give him praise and reward him. Continue practicing this until your puppy can do it ten times in a row, throughout the day.

You can also teach a hand signal (and get pup to drop it for nothing) with an empty hand. Pretend that you have a treat in your hand and present your puppy with the item as you did before. Tell pup to drop it. When he opens his mouth, show him your empty hand. Do this until your puppy associates the empty hand motion with the drop it command.

Leave It

Leave it is a command that is often used with drop it. However, this is used before your puppy picks something up, as she becomes curious with something. This could be a piece of old food, a magnet, or something dangerous like medication or a battery

Step 1: Teach Pup to Leave a Treat

To teach leave it, start by hiding a treat in either fist. Place one of your fists out and allow your dog to sniff it. Most likely, she will smell the treat inside. If she looks away, give her the treat from the other hand and say leave it. Continue to practice this until your pup looks away every time you offer her your fist.

Step 2: Increase Pup's Temptation

Then, practice the exercise with your hand opened this time. Allow your puppy to see the treat, but move your fist away if she tries to get it, telling her to leave it. Do this until your puppy ignores the treat and then reward with the treat from your other hand.

Step 3: Get Pup to Leave it With More Temptation

Next, place a treat on the floor. Give your puppy the command to leave it. If your puppy tries to get the treat, use your hand to cover it. Reward with a different treat once your puppy looks away.

Step 4: Improve Pup's Skill

When your pup instantly responds when the leave it command is given, put a treat on the carpet and put your pup on a leash. Walk past the treat and say leave it. Reward if your puppy listens. If not, be ready to grab the treat. Then, start to practice with real items in your home.

Congratulations! You have reached the end of the section on obedience training and likely have a well-behaved puppy (or young dog) at your side. While the obedience part of the book is over, you can read on to the next chapter if you want to learn some tricks that you can teach your puppy.

Chapter 13: Bonus Chapter: Teaching Your Puppy Tricks

You should note that your puppy is not going to be little anymore by the time he or she is ready to learn tricks. These tricks will range from simple to more advanced. You should definitely teach the advanced tricks once your puppy has some of the more basic ones down to have the best chance at training success.

Hug

The hug command is one that is incredibly cute. After all, who doesn't want a hug from their adorable ball of fluff? For this trick, your puppy will put his paws around you and squeeze.

Step 1: Have Pup Sit

Start by having your puppy sit down, ensuring that he is sitting flat and not leaning toward one side or the other.

Step 2: Get Pup to Let You Handle His Paws

Gently pick up your puppy's paws, paying attention to if he growls. If so, you will want to work on handling your puppy's paws before you try teaching him this trick.

Step 3: Teaching the Hug Command

If your puppy is comfortable with you handling his paws, you will set them on your shoulders and give the command hug, immediately giving your pup a treat.

Step 4: Release Pup and Help Him Get Down

Use a release word after a few seconds and help your puppy get his feet back on the ground. Give your puppy plenty of praise and another treat if you would like.

Dance

The command to dance is similar to the one to hug, since your puppy will be putting her paws on your shoulders. Instead of just hugging, however, your puppy will walk on her hind legs to move around or dance with you. You will find it useful if your puppy knows how to hug before teaching this command.

Step 1: Have Pup Sit and Position Yourself

Start by having your puppy sit down. You will need to kneel

next to her or stand, depending on how big your pup is. Once pup is sitting, give the hug command.

Step 2: Get Your Puppy to Put Her Paws on Your Shoulders

If your puppy does not know the hug command, you can set her paws gently on your shoulders as you did before, giving a treat.

Step 3: Dance with Pup

Once your pup's paws are on your shoulders, give the command to dance. Take 1 small step backward, making your puppy take a step forward. Take a couple steps in this manner, giving your puppy a reward.

Step 4: Release and Reward Your Pup

You should only practice a few steps at a time, until your puppy's hind legs are strong enough to support her standing for a long period of time. When you are finished dancing with your puppy, give the release command and reward with a treat.

Balance

It can be very cute when your puppy balances a treat or bone on her nose and then waits for your command to go after it. This, however, is a trick that must be taught after your puppy is used to having her nose/muzzle area being touched.

Step 1: Get Pup Used to Pleasant Muzzle Experiences

To gauge your pup's reaction, touch your hand to her muzzle and give her a treat, creating a positive experience related to having her muzzle touched.

Step 2: Choose an Item for Pup to Balance

Then, you will want to choose an item for your puppy to balance. You are going to find that your pup will be more likely to balance a toy or another object than she will treats.

Step 3: Briefly Introduce the Object to Your Puppy's Muzzle

Set the balancing item on your pup's nose briefly, just enough that she gets a feel for it and then immediately reward with a treat. Continue to do this until your pup seems to be comfortable, gradually increasing the amount of time that the object is on your puppy's nose.

Step 4: Teaching the Balance Command

Start to give the command balance when you place the object on her nose. One she is familiar with this and can hold the object for a decent period of time, use the same technique but place a treat on your pup's nose instead.

Rollover

In this trick, your puppy will roll over. This is a good trick to teach your puppy before teaching her to play dead, because it familiarizes her with the rolling motion. Your pup must know how to lie down before she will be able to do this trick.

Step 1: Have Your Puppy Lay Down and Entice with a Treat

Once your dog is in a laying position, hold a treat in front of your pup's nose. Pull it forward toward your pup's shoulder; she should turn her head to continue watching the treat.

Step 2: Teaching the Rollover Motion

Continue to pull the treat around your puppy's shoulders, making her lie down on her side. Then, move the treat fully around your pup's body, forcing him to complete an entire roll and then rewarding with praise and a good treat.

Step 3: Get Pup to Rollover Without the Treat

Continue to practice this and add the phrase roll over once your puppy understands the motion. Eventually, she will relate the two. You will know pup has learned this command when she does it upon hearing the command, without the need to be tempted by a treat.

Step 4: Troubleshooting the Technique

If you cannot get your puppy to roll over completely on the first time, break it up into smaller steps. Start by getting your puppy to roll on her side and giving a treat. Then, offer a belly rub or a good scratch if your puppy lies on her back. Finally, use the treat method to try to get your puppy to roll over completely.

Sit Pretty

Sit pretty, also called beg, is a cute trick where your pup will sit on its bottom and put its paws in front of him. Not only is it a cute trick, it helps increase your puppy's balance and can be very useful if your puppy is having trouble standing on his hind legs when you give the command to hug or dance.

Step 1: Have Your Dog Sit

The first step to sitting pretty is getting your pup in the sit position. Tell your pup to sit.

Step 2: Entice Pup with a Treat

Take a treat and hold it slightly in front of your pup's nose. Pull the treat upward. Most likely, your puppy will lift his front feet from the ground as he stretches up to get the treat.

Step 3: Reward Pup and Teach Him to Stand Taller

As soon as your pup lifts is feet from the ground, reward him with a treat and give the command sit pretty. Then, get another treat and use it to make pup stand taller, until he is up on his hind legs.

Play Dead

When your puppy does this fun trick, he will lie down on the floor, roll over on his side, and then relax until you give him the release word. It is essential that your puppy know the lie down command before you teach him to play dead.

Step 1: Have Your Pup Lay on the Ground and Get Him on His Side

Start by having puppy lie down. Take a treat and place it close to your puppy's nose. Slowly pull the treat toward your puppy's side, making it necessary for him to roll over. You will find that it is helpful if your pup already knows this trick as well, since the movement will be familiar.

Step 2: Treat Pup and Lengthen the Time on His Side

Give your puppy a treat as soon as he is on his side. Do this several times and then gradually lengthen the amount of time that he is lying down before you release him and give him the treat.

Step 3: Teach the Play Dead Command

As you increase the time, start to say play dead as your puppy does the motion. With practice, he will start doing this on his own when you tell him to play dead.

Catch

Teaching your puppy to catch is relatively easy, since they will instinctually lunge after a ball or treat to catch it. The ideal training method is to use a small treat, since larger treats and toys may hit your puppy in the face and turn him off of catching before he has even learned the trick.

Step 1: Toss the Item to Pup

Take your small treat and throw it toward your dog's face, aiming a few inches from his nose. If he is successful, say the command catch and reward your pup by letting him have the treat.

Step 2: Take Away the Treat if Pup Does Not Catch the Item

If your puppy fails to catch the treat, try to scoop it up before he does. Otherwise, you will not have a snack to encourage him to learn the trick. You should practice this a handful of times each day and your pup should master catch in no time at all.

Speak

The speak command is used to make your puppy bark, either once or more. You can also teach your pup to speak loud or soft, which will change the volume that your puppy barks at.

Step 1: Get Pup to Bark

If you know what is likely to make your pup bark, then training this command is rather easy. Start by doing something that typically makes your puppy bark, like ringing the doorbell.

Step 2: Teach the Speak Command

As soon as your puppy does bark, give the command speak and reward with a treat. After you have done this a few times, it is likely that your puppy will start to correlate the speak command with barking.

Step 3: Teach Pup to Speak Loudly or Softly

You can train your puppy to speak either loudly or softly as well. Use the same technique, except add the word loud or soft after you give the speak command, depending on how loud your pup is when she barks.

Shake Paws

This command is sometimes said as shake, however, if you have trained your puppy to shake his body with this command, you will need to add paws to it or use a different command phrase. As its name suggests, this command will have your pup shake his paw with the person giving the command.

Step 1: Have Pup Sit and Get Her Interested in the Treat

Start by having your puppy sit. Once she is seated, show her a treat that is in one hand. Close your fist so your pup cannot reach the treat. Keep your hand closed but close to pup's nose, ensuring that she is interested in the treat.

Step 2: Get Pup to Paw Your Hand

Eventually, it is likely that your puppy will try to dig for the treat in your hand. When she brings up her paw to touch you, saying the command shake and reward her by opening your hand and giving praise. Eventually, start to hold pup's paw and shake as you give the command.

Step 3: Troubleshooting the Technique

If your puppy does not paw at your hand to get the treat, position your hand so it is closer to her paw. You can even nudge your puppy's paw if necessary. Once your pup releases her leg so that her paw touches your hand, give her praise and reward.

Spin

The spin command tells your puppy to spin in a circle, as he would when chasing his tail.

Step 1: Give the Spin Command as Your Puppy is Chasing His Tail

The key to easily training this trick is to teach the command when your puppy is already chasing his tail, which pups and dogs may do when they are bored. If this does not work, however, you can still train the command by getting your puppy to follow a treat.

Step 2: Have Pup Stand

It will be useful if your puppy knows the stand command, though you can also train him this if he knows sit. Begin by having your puppy get into the stand position (or sitting, if he cannot stand).

Step 3: Get Pup Interested in the Treat

Take the treat and hold it in your hand, showing it to your puppy and then closing it so he cannot get it. Place your closed fist a few inches in front of your pup's nose, enticing him with the treat.

Step 4: Use the Treat so Pup Makes a Circle and Reward Him

Move your hand around so that he has to stand up and move in a circle to get to the treat. Accompany this action with the command spin. When your pup does a full rotation, reward him with the treat.

Fetch

Even though fetch sounds as if it would be an easy trick to teach your puppy, it is not. Despite puppies having the drive to please their human and a natural desire to chase things, fetch is not something that most pups catch on to easily. This section will teach you what you need to know to help your puppy learn fetch, even if they are struggling with it.

Step 1: Teaching Your Puppy to Chase

The first thing that you are going to do is teach your puppy to chase something. In some cases, you may find that your pup sits and stares at you blankly, in a state of confusion as to why you would through a perfectly good toy away. Start by deciding what the most valuable reward is in your pup's eyes, whether it is affection, treats, or play time. Toss the item on the ground, close to where you are standing with your pup. If he touches his nose to the object to sniff it or put his mouth on it, say fetch and reward him. Continue the process, gradually increasing the distance that you throw the object.

Step 2: Give Pup Resistance

As your puppy continues forward to give chase, you can start to hold your puppy back once you throw the item. Grab onto his collar for a few seconds after you throw the toy, restraining him from giving chase. Say fetch as you let go of your puppy's collar.

Step 3: Teaching Pup to Bring the Item Back

The next part of teaching your puppy to fetch is teaching

your puppy to bring the thrown object back to you. For some pups, this could be accomplished by calling your pup back to you. For others, you may need to tempt him with a second toy or a treat to get him to come to you. Your puppy may drop the first object he was retrieving, but you should still reward him for the motion of running back to you after you say fetch. A third option is to attach a rope to the object you are throwing and pull it towards you when your pup gets it in his mouth. It can be useful to teach a command like all the way or bring it back as your pup learns this part of the technique.

Step 4: Have Puppy Drop the Item

Finally, you are going to teach your puppy to drop the item on command. It will be useful if your puppy already knows the command drop it. You can find instructions for teaching this in the previous chapter. When your pup brings the item back, command him to drop it. If he refuses, place a treat above his nose. In most cases, your puppy will drop the item for the treat. The final advancement of this trick is testing what your pup has been taught with an object that he is fond of.

Fetch Items

Once you have taught your puppy the fetch command, you will eventually have the option of sending your puppy to fetch certain items for you. For example, you may send her to fetch your slippers in the morning or go outside and fetch the newspaper.

Step 1: Teach Pup to Fetch

Once your puppy knows the fetch command, you will find that the key is having your puppy relate the word for whatever you are trying to have her fetch to the item.

Step 2: Put Pup on a Leash and Lead Her to the Item

If you are trying to get your puppy to fetch the newspaper, for example, put your pup on a leash and walk her out toward the newspaper. Give her the command to fetch the newspaper as you place it in her mouth.

Step 3: Getting Pup to Fetch and Bring You the Item

After you have worked on identifying the item, you will want to give your puppy a chance to fetch it and bring it back to you. Use the same commands that you did while training fetch to make training easier and prevent any confusion.

Jump

Before you decide to teach your puppy this or any of the other jumping tricks in this book, there are some considerations to make. First, puppies should not be encouraged to jump because their bones are not yet very strong and they could develop hip problems in the future. Second, older dogs who have a history of hip dysplasia or other hip problems should not be taught these tricks, because it can lead to injury.

Step 1: Entice Your Puppy with a Stick

The easiest way to teach jump is with a stick, though you can use your hand and a treat if you cannot get your puppy interested in the stick. Take the stick and wave it in front of your dog.

Step 2: Get Pup to Jump

Once your dog is interested in the stick, move it upward slowly but swiftly. As your puppy moves up to get it, raise it high enough that he has to jump. If his hind legs come up off the ground, give the command jump and reward with a treat.

Step 3: Troubleshooting the Technique

If your dog seems reluctant to jump up to get the stick, start by having the puppy touch her nose to the stick closer to the ground. Each time she grabs the stick, reward her with a treat and continually move the stick higher until pup is ready to jump.

Step 4: Getting Your Puppy to Jump on Command

With time, your puppy is going to relate the motion of jumping with the command jump. You will eventually want to stop using the jump stick to tempt your puppy.

Jumping Rope

If your puppy knows how to jump, then you can easily teach

the command to jump rope.

Step 1: Getting Pup to Jump Over a Stick

Start by having your puppy stand and stay. Turn around and face your pup, putting a cane to one side of his body. On the other side of the cane, have a treat visible in your hand. Slowly move your cane under pup's feet, giving him the command to jump. Give him the treat when he is on the other side.

Step 2: Do Several Repetitions

Have your puppy jump over the cane or stick 2-3 times. Eventually, you will add more repetitions to the trick as your puppy becomes accustomed to the movement. This is when you will be able to exchange the stick for a jump rope.

Step 3: Give Pup a Treat When You Are Done

Eventually, you will want to space out the treats that you give your puppy. Try giving a treat only at the end of your repetitions with pup.

Teaching Your Pup to Jump through a Hoop

This cool trick involves your puppy jumping through a hula-hoop. It can be fun to teach, but also essential if you plan on having your pup compete in agility training.

Step 1: Choose a Distraction-Free Area and Let Your Puppy Get Comfortable

It will be incredibly hard to teach this trick with distractions, so you should choose an area like a fenced in yard that is free of your pup's toys to teach this trick. Allow your puppy the chance to sniff around and get comfortable. You may also want to show your puppy the hula hoop and let her check it out for a moment, just to be familiar enough that she knows it won't hurt her.

Step 2: Tempt Your Puppy with a Treat to Go Through the Hoop

Before you teach your puppy to jump through the hoop, you are going to get her to walk through the hoop. Give your pup the stand command and have her wait for your direction. Place the hula-hoop in front of her with the treat on the other side. Your puppy should reach for the treat. Continue to pull the treat forward until your pup's hind legs and tail are through the hoop and immediately reward.

Step 3: Add the Jump Command

Next, you are going to add the jump command to your training. Hold the hula-hoop slightly above ground level in front of your puppy with a treat on the other side. Give the command to jump. If you have worked on jump with your puppy, she will jump through the hoop. Give pup a treat and continue to practice this, gradually increasing the height of the hoop from the ground. However, be careful not to put the hoop too high for your puppy and stop immediately if she becomes uncomfortable.

Agility Course Training

Agility training is a great way to bond with your puppy, as well as being great exercise. Often, owners who teach agility training may have their puppy compete in agility courses for prizes. This section will go over how to make the different elements of an agility course to easily practice at home and the technique you should use to train your puppy.

Creating Obstacles for Your Puppy to Practice at Home

Agility training involves getting your pup to go through a number of obstacles. Here is how you can make each one:

- **Weave Poles**- You can use PVC piping or ski poles to easily make weave poles. Stick 10-15 of these in the ground, being sure to leave enough space in between the sets so your puppy can easily weave through them.

- **Standard Jumps**- To make standard jumps, assemble two stacks of cinderblocks to the same height. Put a piece of plywood in between. Remember to only stack as high as your puppy can safely jump.

- **Teeter Boards**- You can create teeterboards using a long piece of wood and PVC piping. Put abrasive strips across the board so that his little paw pads have something to grip onto as he walks. Make 2 holes in the PVC piping, one on either side off the pipe. Attach carriage bolts to the board and then thread these through the PVC piping. Tightly screw the nuts on the inside of the pipe for a sturdy teeterboard.

- **Pause Table**- You can build your own pause table or you can use a coffee table. Choose or build a table that sits low to the ground, being sure that it is sturdy enough to support your pup's weight.

- **Dogwalk**- You can use the bench from a picnic table for a dogwalk, or you can make one by setting two cinderblocks a little less than 12-feet apart and setting a 12-foot piece of plywood across them.

- **Tire Jump**- Use an old car tire or bike tire and hang it from a sturdy tree branch. As you choose the tire, be sure your puppy can safely fit through it. You will want to hold onto this as you teach your pup, to stop him from hitting the sides and being scared at first.

- **Tunnel**- The easiest way to find a tunnel is to purchase a collapsible kid's toy tunnel. In most cases, this will be less than $20 and it is a lot easier than finding the parts to construct your own.

Technique to Get Puppy through the Course

If you have made it this far in the book, hopefully you have already taught many of the tricks up to this point. If so, then it will be significantly easier to train your puppy to go through the course. You should note that you must take agility training slow, often focusing on a single part of the course each day until your puppy is comfortable doing everything.

Many of these tricks are difficult, so you should choose a high-value treat to give your pup as he goes through the course. For some of the tricks (like weave poles), you will want to use the treat in your hand. For other obstacles (like the tunnels), you may want to attach the treat to the end of a pole, since your arm will not be long enough to tempt pup to come through.

You are going to focus on getting your puppy to learn each of the obstacles before focusing on agility. As you have pup practice each part, be sure to assign it a name and reward with a treat at the end. Be patient as you guide pup through the course and you will be working on improving speed and agility in no time at all.

Conclusion

If you have reached this point then congratulations! You now possess all the knowledge that you need to raise a 7-week old puppy into a healthy, well-mannered dog.

The next logical step is to put what you have been taught to the test. You will find that not only that your puppy is receptive, but also that he or she is easier to train since you know exactly what to do.

As you train your puppy, remember to teach the basics first and then build upon what your pup already knows. Additionally, make sure that you are consistent and that everyone in your household (as well as guests to the home) is onboard with training your pup.

Training a puppy is a lot of work, but with the right techniques you will find that it is not nearly as difficult as it is made out to be. This is especially true since puppies are nearly clean slates, ready and willing to learn when they have the right leadership and direction.

As you train your puppy, stay consistent and perseverant. Your hard work will pay off when your pup has grown into a dog that you can trust to roam your home when you are not around and even sleep outside of his cage at night.

Made in the USA
San Bernardino, CA
03 December 2017